Introduction to Networking

Charles Severance

Credits

Illustrations: Mauro Toselli
Editorial Support: Sue Blumenberg
Cover Design: Aimee Andrion

The SketchNote illustrations were drawn on an iPad using *Paper* by www.fiftythree.com using a dedicated stylus pencil. The illustrations were converted from PNG to SVG and EPS vector formats using www.vectormagic.com. The technical figures for the book were drawn with OmniGraffle.

Printing History

2015-May-25 Original Printing - CreateSpace

Copyright Details

Preface

The goal of this book is to provide a basic understanding of the technical design and architecture of the Internet. The book is aimed at all audiences – even those with absolutely no prior technical experience or math skills. The Internet is an amazingly beautiful design and should be understood by all who use it.

While this book is not about the Network+ or CCNA certifications, I hope it serves as a way to give students interested in these certifications a good starting point.

I want to thank Pamela Fox of Khan Academy for coming up with the idea of an introductory network technology course using open materials.

I initially developed this material as a single week's lecture in the *SI502 - Networked Computing* course that I taught at the University of Michigan School of Information starting in 2008. I refined and expanded the material to be three weeks of the Internet History, Technology, and Security (IHTS) course that I have taught to over 100,000 students on Coursera starting in 2012. This book adds further detail to create a standalone text that can be read for enjoyment or used to support an introductory course that focuses on the Internet's architecture.

This book has been particularly fun in that it is a collaboration with my friends Mauro Toselli (@xlontrax) and Sue Blumenberg. I met Mauro and Sue in 2012 when they became volunteer Community Teaching Assistants (CTAs) for my IHTS course on Coursera. Over the past three years we have become friends and colleagues. It is a great example of how open education can bring people together.

There is supporting material for this book at

http://www.net-intro.com/

If you like the book, let us know. Send us a tweet with your thoughts. You can also send a tweet if you find an error in the book.

Charles R. Severance (@drchuck)
www.dr-chuck.com
Ann Arbor, MI USA
May 20, 2015

Contents

Chapter 1

Introduction

Using the Internet seems pretty easy. We go to a web address and up comes a page. Or we go to our favorite social site and see pictures of our friends, families, and pets. But it takes a lot of complex software and hardware to make the Internet seem so simple. The design of the technologies that make today's Internet work started in the 1960s, and there were over 20 years of research into how to build internetworking technologies before the first "Internet" was built in the late 1980s by academics in a project called NSFNet. Since then, the research and development into improving network technologies has continued as networks have become far larger and faster and globally distributed with billions of computers.

In order to better understand how today's Internet works, we will take a look at how humans and computers have communicated using technology over the years.

1.1   Communicating at a Distance

Imagine a group of five people in a room sitting in a circle. As long as they are courteous and don't have more than one conversation at the same time, it's quite natural for any person to talk to any other person in the room. They just need to be able to hear each other and coordinate how to use the shared space in the room.

But what if we put these people in different rooms so they can no longer see or hear each other? How could pairs of people communicate with each other then? One way might be to run a wire between each pair of people with a microphone on one end and a speaker on the other end. Now everyone could still hear all

1

the conversations. They would still need to be courteous to make sure that there was only one conversation going on at the same time.

Each person would need four speakers (one for each of the other people) and enough pieces of wire to connect all the microphones and speakers. This is a problem with five people and it gets far worse when there are hundreds or thousands of people.

Using wires, microphones, and speakers is how early telephone systems from the 1900s allowed people to make phone calls. Because they could not have separate wires between every pair of telephones, these systems did not allow all pairs of people to be connected at the same time. Each person had a single connection to a human "operator". The operator would connect two wires together to allow a pair of people to talk, and then disconnect them when the conversation was finished.

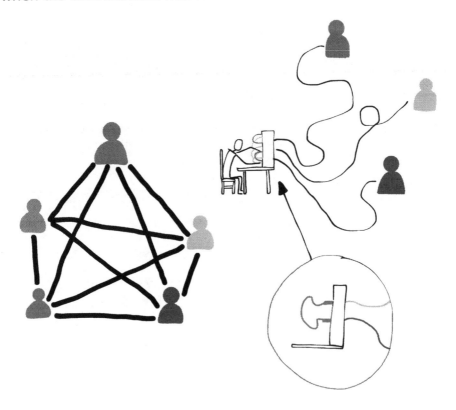

Figure 1.1: Connecting Using Telephone Operators

The first local telephone systems worked well when a customer's home or business was close to the operator's building and a wire could be strung directly from the operator's building to the person's home.

But what if thousands people who are hundreds of kilometers apart need to be able to communicate? We can't run 100-kilometer wires from each home to a single central office. What the telephone companies did instead was to have many central offices and run a few wires between the central offices, then share connections between central offices. For long distances, a connection might run through a number of central offices. Before the advent of fiber optic, long-distance telephone calls were carried between cities on poles with lots of separate wires. The number of wires on the poles represented the number of possible simultaneous long-distance phone calls that could use those wires.

Figure 1.2: Long-Distance Telephone Poles

Since the cost of the wires went up as the length of the wire increased, these longer connections between offices were quite expensive to install and maintain, and they were scarce. So in the early days of telephones, local calls were generally quite inexpensive. But long-distance calls were more expensive and they were charged by the minute. This made sense because each minute you talked on a long-distance call, your use of the long-distance wires meant no one else could use them. The telephone companies wanted you to keep your calls short so their long-distance lines would be available for other customers.

When telephone companies started using fiber optic, more advanced techniques were used to carry many simultaneous long-distance conversations on a single fiber. When you look at an old photo and see lots of wires on a single pole, it generally means they were telephone wires and not used to carry electricity.

1.2 Computers Communicate Differently

When humans talk on the phone, they make a call, talk for a while, and then hang up. Statistically, most of the time, humans are not talking on the phone. At least they weren't before everyone had smartphones. But computers, including the applications on your smartphone, communicate differently than humans do. Sometimes computers send short messages to check if another computer is available. Computers sometimes send medium-sized information like a single picture or a long email message. And sometimes computers send a lot of information like a whole movie or a piece of software to install that might take minutes or even hours to download. So messages between computers can be short, medium, or long.

In the earliest days of connecting computers to one another, pairs of computers were connected with wires. The simplest way to send data from one computer to another was to line up the outgoing messages in a queue and send the messages one after another as fast as the computers and the wires could carry the data. Each message would wait for its turn until the messages ahead of it were sent, and then it would get its chance to be sent across the connection.

When the computers were in the same building, the building owner could run wires to connect them. If the computers were in the same town, the owners of the computers generally had to lease wires from the telephone companies to connect their computers. They often would have the phone company connect the wires together in their central office so that it was not necessary for one computer to "dial" the other computer to send data. These leased lines were convenient for computer communications because they were "always on", but they were also quite expensive because they were used 24 hours a day.

When the computers were even farther away, in different cities, the leased lines were extended using the longer wires connecting the central offices. Since there were so few wires between central offices, these long-distance leased lines were quite expensive and their cost increased dramatically as the length of the leased line increased. But if you had enough money, you could lease direct connections between your computers so they could exchange data. This worked pretty well as long as you were only using one brand of computers, because each computer company had their own way of using telephone wires to connect their computers together and send data.

1.3 Early Wide Area Store-and-Forward Networks

In the 1970s and 1980s, people working at universities around the world wanted to send each other data and messages using these computer-to-computer connections. Since the cost for each connection was so high and increased with distance, computers generally only had connections to other nearby computers. But if the computer that you were connected to was connected to another computer and that computer in turn was connected to another computer, and so on, you could send a message a long distance as long as each of the computers along the route of the message agreed to store and forward your message.

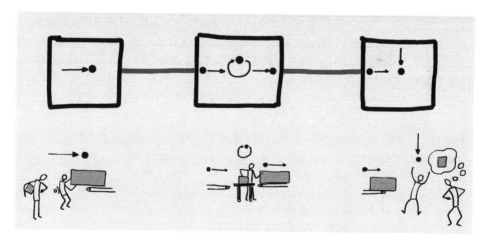

Figure 1.3: Store-and-Forward Networks

Over time, with relatively few connections you could send data long distances across a patchwork of network connections as long as you were patient. Along the way, after your message reached one computer, it would have to wait until its turn came to be sent to the next computer along the route. A message would arrive at an intermediate computer, be stored for a while (perhaps hours, depending on traffic), and then be forwarded one more connection (or "hop").

Sending entire messages one at a time this way, a message might take minutes, hours, or even days to arrive at its ultimate destination, depending on the traffic at each of the hops. But even if it took a few hours for an email message to find its way from one part of the country to another, this was still much quicker and easier than sending a letter or postcard.

1.4 Packets and Routers

The most important innovation that allowed messages to move more quickly across a multi-hop network was to break each message into small fragments and send each fragment individually. In networking terms, these pieces of messages are called "packets". The idea of breaking a message into packets was pioneered in the 1960s, but it was not widely used until the 1980s because it required more computing power and more sophisticated networking software.

When messages are broken into packets and each packet is sent separately, if a short message was sent after a large message had begun, the short message did not have to wait until the entire long message was finished. The first packet of the short message only had to wait for the current packet of the large message to be finished. The system alternated sending packets from the long and short messages until after a while the short message was completely sent and the long message resumed making full use of the network connection.

Breaking the message into packets also greatly reduced the amount of storage needed in the intermediate computers because instead of needing to store an entire message for as long as a few hours, the intermediate computer only needed to store a few packets for a few seconds while the packets waited for their turns on the outbound link.

As networks moved away from the store-and-forward approach, they started to include special-purpose computers that specialized in moving packets. These were initially called "Interface Message Processors" or "IMPs" because they acted as the interface between general-purpose computers and the rest of the network. Later these computers dedicated to communications were called "routers" because their purpose was to route the packets they received towards their ultimate destination.

By building routers that specialized in moving packets across multiple hops, it became simpler to connect computers from multiple

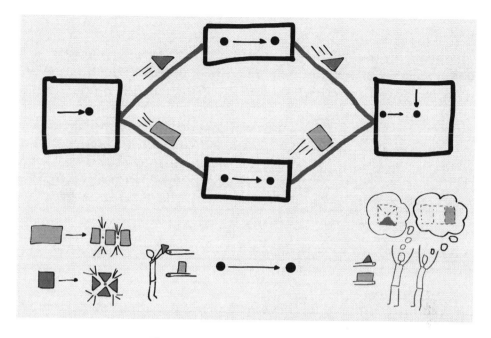

Figure 1.4: Sending Packets

vendors to the same network. To connect any computer to the network, now all you needed to do was connect it to one router and then the rest of the communication details were handled by the other routers.

When multiple computers at one location were connected to-gether in a "Local Area Network" (or LAN) using physical wiring, you would connect a router to the local area network. By sending data through the router, all the computers on the local area network could send data across the "Wide Area Network" (or WAN).

1.5 Addressing and Packets

In the early store-and-forward networks it was important to know the source and destination computers for every message. Each computer was given a unique name or number that was called the "address" of the computer. To send a message to another computer, you needed to add the source and destination address to the message before sending the message along its way. By having a source and destination address in each message, the computers that stored and forwarded the message would be able to pick the best path for the message if more than one path was available.

When a long message was split into much smaller packets and each packet was sent individually, the source and destination addresses had to be added to each packet, so that routers could choose the best path to forward each packet of the message. In addition to the source and destination addresses, it was also necessary to add data to each packet indicating the "offset" or position of the packet in the overall message so that the receiving computer could put the packets back together in the right order to reconstruct the original message.

1.6 Putting It All Together

So when we combine all this together we can understand the basic operation of today's Internet. We have specialized computers called "routers" that know how to route packets along a path from a source to a destination. Each packet will pass through multiple routers during its journey from the source computer to the destination computer.

Even though the packets may be part of a larger message, the routers forward each packet separately based on its source and destination addresses. Different packets from the same message may take different routes from the source to the destination. And sometimes packets even arrive out of order; a later packet might arrive before an earlier packet, perhaps because of a data "traffic jam". Each packet contains an "offset" from the beginning of the message so that the destination computer can reassemble the packets in the correct order to reconstruct the original message.

By creating a network using multiple short hops, the overall cost of communicating across a large geographical area could be spread across a large number of connecting groups and individuals. Normally, packets would find the shortest path between the source and destination, but if a link on that path was an overloaded or broken, the routers could cooperate and reroute traffic to take slightly longer paths that would get packets from a source to a destination as quickly as possible.

The core of the Internet is a set of cooperating routers that move packets from many sources to many destinations at the same time. Each computer or local area network is connected to a router that forwards the traffic from its location to the various destinations on the Internet. A router might handle data from a single

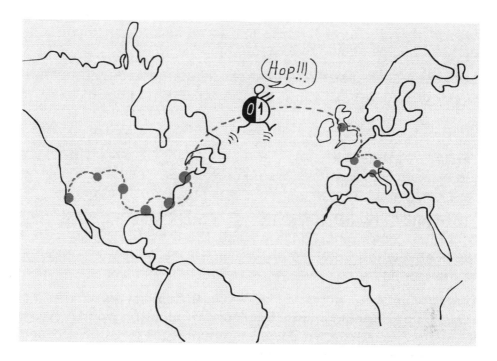

Figure 1.5: Connecting Around the World

computer like a smartphone, from several computers in the same building, or from thousands of computers connected to a university campus network. The term "Internet" comes from the idea of "internetworking", which captures the idea of connecting many networks together. Our computers connect to local networks and the Internet connects the local networks together so all of our computers can talk to each other.

1.7 Glossary

address: A number that is assigned to a computer so that messages can be routed to the computer.

hop: A single physical network connection. A packet on the Internet will typically make several "hops" to get from its source computer to its destination.

LAN: Local Area Network. A network covering an area that is limited by the ability for an organization to run wires or the power of a radio transmitter.

leased line: An "always up" connection that an organization leased from a telephone company or other utility to send data across longer distances.

operator (telephone): A person who works for a telephone company and helps people make telephone calls.

packet: A limited-size fragment of a large message. Large messages or files are split into many packets and sent across the
Internet. The typical maximum packet size is between 1000 and
3000 characters.

router: A specialized computer that is designed to receive incoming packets on many links and quickly forward the packets on the
best outbound link to speed the packet to its destination.

store-and-forward network: A network where data is sent
from one computer to another with the message being stored
for relatively long periods of time in an intermediate computer
waiting for an outbound network connection to become available.

WAN: Wide Area Network. A network that covers longer distances, up to sending data completely around the world. A WAN
is generally constructed using communication links owned and
managed by a number of different organizations.

1.8 Questions

You can take this quiz online at http://www.net-intro.com/quiz/

1. What did early telephone operators do?

   a) Maintained cell phone towers
   b) Connected pairs of wires to allow people to talk
   c) Installed copper wire between cities
   d) Sorted packets as they went to the correct destination

2. What is a leased line?

   a) A boundary between leased and owned telephone equip-
      ment
   b) A connection between a keyboard and monitor
   c) A wire that ran from one phone company office to another
   d) An "always on" telephone connection

3. How long might a message be stored in an intermediate computer for a store-and-forward network?

a) less than a second
b) no more than four seconds
c) less than a minute
d) possibly as long as several hours

4. What is a packet?

a) A technique for wrapping items for shipping
b) A small box used for storage
c) A portion of a larger message that is sent across a network
d) The amount of data that could be stored on an early punched card

5. Which of these is most like a router?

a) A mail sorting facility
b) A refrigerator
c) A high-speed train
d) An undersea telecommunications cable

6. What was the name given to early network routers?

a) Interfaith Message Processors
b) Internet Motion Perceptrons
c) Instant Message Programs
d) Interface Message Processors

7. In addition to breaking large messages into smaller segments to be sent, what else was needed to properly route each message segment?

a) A source and destination address on each message segment
b) An ID and password for each message segment
c) A small battery to maintain the storage for each message segment
d) A small tracking unit like a GPS to find lost messages

8. Why is it virtually free to send messages around the world using the Internet?

a) Because governments pay for all the connections
b) Because advertising pays for all the connections
c) Because so many people share all the resources
d) Because it is illegal to charge for long-distance connections

Chapter 2

Network Architecture

To engineer and build a system as complex as the Internet, engineers try to break a single challenging problem into a set of smaller problems that can be solved independently and then put back together to solve the original large problem. The engineers who built the first internets broke the overall problem into four basic subproblems that could be worked on independently by different groups.

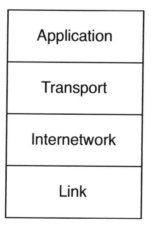

Figure 2.1: The Four-Layer TCP/IP Model

They gave these four areas of engineering the following names: (1) Link, (2) Internetwork, (3) Transport, and (4) Application. We visualize these different areas as layers stacked on top of each other, with the Link layer on the bottom and the Application layer on the top. The Link layer deals with the wired or wireless connection from your computer to the local area network and the Application layer is what we as end users interact with. A web browser is one example of an application in this Internet architecture.

We informally refer to this model as the "TCP/IP model" in reference to the Transport Control Protocol (TCP) used to implement the Transport layer and Internet Protocol (IP) used to implement the Internetwork layer.

We will take a quick look at each of the layers, starting from the "bottom" of the stack.

2.1   The Link Layer

The Link layer is responsible for connecting your computer to its local network and moving the data across a single hop. The most common Link layer technology today is wireless networking. When you are using a wireless device, the device is only sending data a limited distance. A smartphone communicates with a tower that is a few kilometers away. If you are using your smartphone on a train, it needs to switch to a new tower every few minutes when the train is moving. A laptop that is connected to a WiFi network is usually communicating with a base station within 200 meters. A desktop computer that is connected using a wired connection is usually using a cable that is 100 meters long or shorter. Link layer technologies are often shared amongst multiple computers at the same location.

The Link layer needs to solve two basic problems when dealing with these shared local area networks. The first problem is how to encode and send data across the link. If the link is wireless, engineers must agree on which radio frequencies are to be used to transmit data and how the digital data is to be encoded in the radio signal. For wired connections, they must agree on what voltage to use on the wire and how fast to send the bits across the wire. For Link layer technologies that use fiber optics, they must agree on the frequencies of light to be used and how fast to send the data.

In addition to agreeing on how to send data using a shared medium such as a wireless network, they also need to agree on how to cooperate with other computers that might want to send data at the same time. If all the computers on the network tried to transmit whenever they had data to send, their messages would collide. The result would be chaos, and receiving stations would only receive noise. So we need to find a fair way to allow each station to wait its turn to use the shared network.

The idea of breaking a large message into packets and then sending each packet separately makes this sharing easier. If only one computer wants to send data, it will send its packets one right another and move its data across the network as quickly as it can. But if three computers want to send data at the same time, each computer will send one packet and then wait while the other two computers send packets. After each of the other computers sends a packet, the first computer will send its next packet. This way the computers are sharing access to the network in a fair way.

But how does a computer know if other computers want to send data at the same time? Engineers designed an ingenious method to solve this problem called "Carrier Sense Multiple Access with Collision Detection", or CSMA/CD. It is a long name for a simple and elegant concept. When your computer wants to send data, it first listens to see if another computer is already sending data on the network (Carrier Sense). If no other computer is sending data, your computer starts sending its data. As your computer is sending data it also listens to see if it can receive its own data. If your computer receives its own data, it knows that the channel is still clear and continues transmitting. But if two computers started sending at about the same time, the data collides, and your computer does not receive its own data. When a collision is detected, both computers stop transmitting, wait a bit, and retry the transmission. The two computers that collided wait different lengths of time to retry their transmissions to reduce the chances of a second collision.

When your computer finishes sending a packet of data, it pauses to give other computers that have been waiting a chance to send data. If another computer senses that your computer has stopped sending data (Carrier Sense) and starts sending its own packet, your computer will detect the other computer's use of the network and wait until that computer's packet is complete before attempting to send its next packet.

This simple mechanism works well when only one computer wants to send data. It also works well when many computers want to send data at the same time. When only one computer is sending data, that computer can make good use of the shared network by sending packets one after another, and when many computers want to use the shared network at the same time, each computer gets a fair share of the link.

Some link layers, like a cellular connection for a smartphone, a WiFi connection, or a satellite or cable modem, are shared con-

Link Layer

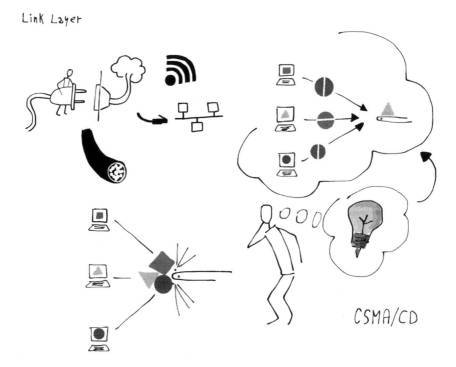

Figure 2.2: Carrier Sense/Collision Detection

nections and need techniques like CSMA/CD to insure fair access to the many different computers connected to the network. Other link layers like fiber optic cables and leased lines are generally not shared and are used for connections between routers. These non-shared connections are still part of the Link layer.

The engineers working on Link layer technologies focus solving the issues so computers can transmit data across a single link that ranges in distance from a few meters to as long as hundreds of kilometers. But to move data greater distances, we need to send our packets through multiple routers connected by multiple link layers. Each time our packet passes through another link layer from one router to another we call it a "hop". To send data halfway around the world, it will pass through about 20 routers, or make 20 "hops".

2.2 The Internetwork Layer (IP)

Once your packet destined for the Internet makes it across the first link, it will be in a router. Your packet has a source address and destination address and the router needs to look at the destination address to figure out how to best move your packet towards its destination. With each router handling packets destined for any of many billions of destination computers, it's not possible for every router to know the exact location and best route to every possible destination computer. So the router makes its best guess as to how to get your packet closer to its destination.

Each of the other routers along the way also does its best to get your packet closer to the destination computer. As your packet gets closer to its final destination, the routers have a better idea of exactly where your packet needs to go. When the packet reaches the last link in its journey, the link layer knows exactly where to send your packet.

We use a similar approach to route ourselves when going on holiday. A holiday trip also has many hops. Perhaps the first hop is driving your car or taking a cab or bus to a train station. Then you take a local train from your small town to a larger city. In the larger city you take a long-distance train to a large city in another country. Then you take another local train to the small village where you will stay for your holiday. When you get off the train, you take a bus, and when you get off the bus, you walk to your hotel.

If you were on the train between the two large cities and you asked the conductor the exact location of your hotel in the small village, the conductor would not know. The conductor only knows how to get you closer to your destination, and while you are on the long-distance train that is all that matters. When you get on the bus at your destination village, you can ask the bus driver which stop is closest to your hotel. And when you get off the bus at the right bus stop, you can probably ask a person on the street where to find the hotel and get an exact answer.

The further you are from your destination, the less you need to know the exact details of how to get there. When you are far away, all you need to know is how to get "closer" to your destination. Routers on the Internet work the same way. Only the routers that are closest to the destination computer know the exact path to that computer. All of the routers in the middle of the journey work to get your message closer to its destination.

But just like when you are traveling, unexpected problems or delays can come up that require a change in plans as your packets are sent across the network.

Routers exchange special messages to inform each other about

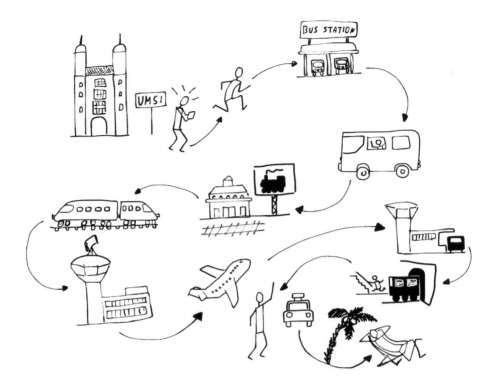

Figure 2.3: A Multi-Step Trip

any kind of traffic delay or network outage so that packets can be switched from a route that is no longer working to a different route. The routers that make up the core of the Internet are smart and adapt quickly to both small and large outages or failures of network connections. Sometimes a connection slows down because it is overloaded. Other times a connection is physically broken when a construction crew mistakenly digs up a buried wire and cuts it. Sometimes there is a natural disaster like a hurricane or typhoon that shuts down the routers and links in a large geographical area. The routers quickly detect these outages and reroute around them if possible.

But sometimes things go wrong and packets are lost. Dealing with lost packets is the reason for the next layer in our architecture.

2.3 The Transport Layer (TCP)

The Internetwork layer is both simple and complex. It looks at a packet's destination address and finds a path across multiple network hops to deliver the packet to the destination computer.

But sometimes these packets get lost or badly delayed. Other times the packets arrive at their destination out of order because a later packet found a quicker path through the network than an earlier packet. Each packet contains the source computer's address, the destination computer's address, and an offset of where this packet "fits" relative to the beginning of the message. Knowing the offset of each packet from the beginning of the message and the length of the packet, the destination computer can reconstruct the original message even if the packets were received out of order.

As the destination computer reconstructs the message and delivers it to the receiving application, it periodically sends an acknowledgement back to the source computer indicating how much of the message it has received and reconstructed. But if the destination computer finds that parts of the reconstructed message are missing, this probably means that these packets were lost or badly delayed. After waiting a bit, the destination computer sends another message to the source computer to resend the missing packet or packets.

The sending computer must store a copy of the parts of the original message that have been sent until the destination computer acknowledges successful receipt of the packets. Once the source computer receives the acknowledgment of successful receipt of a portion of the message, it can discard the data that has been acknowledged and send some more data.

The amount of data that the source computer sends before waiting for an acknowledgement is called the "window size". If the window size is too small, the data transmission is slowed because the source computer is always waiting for acknowledgments. If the source computer sends too much data before waiting for an acknowledgment, it can unintentionally cause traffic problems by overloading routers or long-distance communication lines. This problem is solved by keeping the window size small at the beginning and timing how long it takes to receive the first acknowledgements. If the acknowledgments come back quickly, the source computer slowly increases the window size and if the acknowledgements come back slowly, the source computer keeps the window size small so as not to overload the network. Just like at the Link layer, a little courtesy on the Internet goes a long way toward ensuring good use of the shared network infrastructure.

This strategy means that when the network has high-speed connections and is lightly loaded the data will be sent quickly, and if the network is heavily loaded or has slow connections the data

will be slowed down to match the limitations of the network connections between the source and destination computers.

2.4 The Application Layer

The Link, Internetwork, and Transport layers work together to
quickly and reliably move data between two computers across
a shared network of networks. With this capability to move data
reliably, the next question is what networked applications will be
built to make use of these network connections.

When the first widely used Internet came into being in the mid-
1980s, the first networked applications allowed users to log in to
remote computers, transfer files between computers, send mail
between computers, and even do real-time text chats between
computers.

In the early 1990s, as the Internet came to more people and computers' abilities to handle images improved, the World Wide Web
application was developed by scientists at the CERN high-energy
physics facility. The web was focused on reading and editing networked hypertext documents with images. Today the web is the
most common network application in use around the world. But
all the other older Internet applications are still in wide use.

Each application is generally broken into two halves. One half of
the application is called the "server". It runs on the destination
computer and waits for incoming networking connections. The
other half of the application is called the "client" and runs on the
source computer. When you are browsing the web using software
like Firefox, Chrome, or Internet Explorer, you are running a "web
client" application which is making connections to web servers
and displaying the pages and documents stored on those web
servers. The Uniform Resource Locators (URLs) that your web
browser shows in its address bar are the web servers that your
client is contacting to retrieve documents for you to view.

When we develop the server half and the client half of a networked application, we must also define an "application protocol"
that describes how the two halves of the application will exchange
messages over the network. The protocols used for each application are quite different and specialized to meet the needs of the
particular application. Later we will explore some of these Application layer protocols.

2.5 Stacking the Layers

We usually show the four different layers (Link, Internetwork, Transport, and Application) stacked on top of each other with the Application layer at the top and the Link layer at the bottom. The reason we show them this way is because each layer makes use of the layers above and below it to achieve networked communications.

All four layers run in your computer where you run the client application (like a browser), and all four layers also run in the destination computer where the application server is running. You as the end user interact with the applications that make up the top layer of the stack, and the bottom layer represents the WiFi, cellular, or wired connection between your computer and the rest of the Internet.

The routers that forward your packets from one to another to move your packets towards their destination have no understanding of either the Transport or Application layers. Routers operate at the Internetwork and Link layers. The source and destination addresses at the Internetwork layer are all that is needed for routers to move your packets across the series of links (hops) to get them to the destination. The Transport and Application layers only come into play after the Internetwork layer delivers your packets to the destination computer.

If you wanted to write your own networked application, you would likely only talk to the Transport layer and be completely unconcerned about the Internetwork and Link layers. They are essential to the function of the Transport layer, but as you write your program, you do not need to be aware of any of the lower-layer details. The layered network model makes it simpler to write networked applications because so many of the complex details of moving data from one computer to another can be ignored.

Up next, we will talk about these four layers in more detail.

2.6 Glossary

client: In a networked application, the client application is the one that requests services or initiates connections.

fiber optic: A data transmission technology that encodes data using light and sends the light down a very long strand of thin glass or plastic. Fiber optic connections are fast and can cover very long distances.

offset: The relative position of a packet within an overall message or stream of data.

server: In a networked application, the server application is the one that responds to requests for services or waits for incoming connections.

window size: The amount of data that the sending computer is allowed to send before waiting for an acknowledgement.

2.7 Questions

You can take this quiz online at http://www.net-intro.com/quiz/

1. Why do engineers use a "model" to organize their approach to solving a large and complex problem?

   a) Because it allows them to build something small and test it in a wind tunnel
   b) Because talking about a model delays the actual start of the hard work
   c) Because they can break a problem down into a set of smaller problems that can be solved independently
   d) Because it helps in developing marketing materials

2. Which is the top layer of the network model used by TCP/IP networks?

   a) Application
   b) Transport
   c) Internetwork
   d) Link

3. Which of the layers concerns itself with getting a packet of data across a single physical connection?

   a) Application
   b) Transport
   c) Internetwork

   d) Link

4. What does CSMA/CD stand for?

   a) Carrier Sense Multiple Access with Collision Detection
   b) Collision Sense Media Access with Continuous Direction
   c) Correlated Space Media Allocation with Constant Division
   d) Constant State Multiple Address Channel Divison

5. What is the goal of the Internetwork layer?

   a) Insure that no data is lost while enroute
   b) Get a packet of data moved across multiple networks from its source to its destination
   c) Make sure that only logged-in users can use the Internet
   d) Insure than WiFi is fairly shared across multiple computers

6. In addition to the data, source, and destination addresses, what else is needed to make sure that a message can be reassembled when it reaches its destination?

   a) An offset of where the packet belongs relative to the beginning of the message
   b) A location to send the data to if the destination computer is down
   c) A compressed and uncompressed version of the data in the packet
   d) The GPS coordinates of the destination computer

7. What is "window size"?

   a) The sum of the length and width of a packet
   b) The maximum size of a single packet
   c) The maximum number of packets that can make up a message
   d) The maximum amount of data a computer can send before receiving an acknowledgement

9. In a typical networked client/server application, where does the client application run?

   a) On your laptop, desktop, or mobile computer

b) On a wireless access point

c) On the closest router

d) In an undersea fiber optic cable

10. What does URL stand for?

a) Universal Routing Linkage

b) Uniform Retransmission Logic

c) Uniform Resource Locator

d) Unified Recovery List

Chapter 3

Link Layer

The lowest layer of our Internet Architecture is the Link layer. We call it the "lowest layer" because it is closest to the physical network media. Often the Link layer transmits data using a wire, a fiber optic cable, or a radio signal. A key element of the Link layer is that usually data can only be transmitted part of the way from the source computer to the destination computer. Wired Ethernet, WiFi, and the cellular phone network are examples of link layers that can transmit data about a kilometer. Fiber optic cables, particularly those under the oceans, can transmit data up to thousands of kilometers. Satellite links can also send data over long distances.

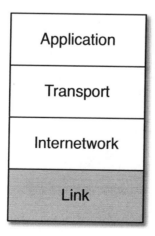

Figure 3.1: The Link Layer

Regardless of the distance we can send the data, it is still traveling over a single link, and to reach the ultimate destination computer requires forwarding packets across multiple links. In this section we will look at how one of the most common link layers functions in some detail. WiFi is a great way to look at many issues that must be solved at the link layer.[1]

3.1 Sharing the Air

When your laptop or phone is using WiFi to connect to the Internet, it is sending and receiving data with a small, low-powered radio. The radio in your computer can only send data about 300 meters, so your computer sends your packets to the router in your home, which forwards the packets using a link to the rest of the Internet. Sometimes we call the first router that handles your computer's packets the "base station" or "gateway".

All computers that are close enough to the base station with their radios turned on receive all of the packets the base station transmits, regardless of which computer the packet is supposed to be sent to. They also "hear" all the packets sent by every other nearby computer. So your computer needs a way to to know which packets to treat as its own and which packets are being sent to other computers and can be safely ignored.

An interesting side effect of the fact that all the computers within range can hear all packets is that a rogue computer could also be listening to and capturing your packets, perhaps getting ahold of important data like bank account numbers or passwords to online services. We will come back to the issue of protecting your data from prying eyes and ears in a later section.

Every WiFi radio in every device that is ever built is given a unique serial number at the time it is manufactured. This means that each of the computers using WiFi has its own serial number, and the radio in the gateway also has a serial number. You can usually go into a settings screen on your device and look up the serial number for the WiFi radio in your device. It is generally shown in the following form:

```
0f:2a:b3:1f:b3:1a
```

This is just a representation of a 48-bit serial number for your WiFi radio. It is also called the "Media Access Control" or "MAC"

---

[1]We simplify some of the technical detail in these descriptions to make them easier to understand.

address. A MAC address is like a "from" or "to" address on a postcard. Every packet (radio postcard) sent across the WiFi has a source and destination address, so all of the computers know which messages are theirs.

When you turn on your computer and connect to a WiFi network, your computer needs to figure out which of the MAC addresses on the WiFi can be used to send packets to the router. When you move from one physical location to another, your computer will be talking to different gateways and each of those gateways will have a different serial number. So when you first connect to a new WiFi, your computer must discover the MAC address for the gateway of that particular WiFi.

To do this, your computer sends a special message to a broadcast address, effectively asking the question, "Who is in charge of this WiFi?" Since your computer knows it is not the gateway itself, it sends a broadcast message with its own serial number as the "from" address and the broadcast address as the "to" address to ask if there are any gateways present on the WiFi network.

```
From: 0f:2a:b3:1f:b3:1a
To: ff:ff:ff:ff:ff:ff
Data: Who is the MAC-Gateway
      for this network?
```

If there is a gateway on the network, the gateway sends a message containing its serial number back to your computer.

```
From: 98:2f:4e:78:c1:b4
To: 0f:2a:b3:1f:b3:1a
Data: I am the gateway
      Welcome to my network
```

If there are no replies, your computer waits a few seconds and then assumes there is no gateway for this network. When there is no gateway, your computer might show a different WiFi icon or not show the WiFi icon at all. Sometimes there can be more than one gateway, but we will ignore that for a while because it is a little complex and not very common.

Once your computer receives a message with the MAC address of the gateway, it can use that address to send packets that it wants the gateway to forward to the Internet. From that point on, all of your computer's packets have the actual serial number of the destination. You want to use the broadcast address as little as possible because every computer connected to the WiFi receives and processes any messages sent to the broadcast address to make sure the messages were not intended for them.

3.2 Courtesy and Coordination

Because many computers are sharing the same radio frequencies, it's important to coordinate how they send data. When there's a crowd of people in a room, they can't all talk at the same time or everything will be garbled. The same thing happens when multiple WiFi radios transmit at the same time on the same frequency. So we need some way to coordinate all the radios to make best use of the shared frequencies. We will look at the basics of technical approaches to avoiding lost data due to transmission "collisions".

The first technique is called "Carrier Sense". The technique is to first listen for a transmission, and if there is already a transmission in progress, wait until the transmission finishes. It might seem like you could wait for a long time, but since all messages are broken into packets, usually your computer only has to wait for the computer currently sending data to finish a packet, after which your computer gets its chance to send data.

If your computer's WiFi radio listens for data and hears silence, it can begin transmitting. But what if another computer's WiFi radio that wants to send a packet listened to and heard the same silence and decided to start transmitting at exactly the same time? If two or more WiFi radios start transmitting at the same time, all of the data is corrupted and both packets are lost. So once your WiFi radio starts sending a packet it is important for it to listen to make sure it can receive its own data. If it is not receiving the same thing that it is sending, your WiFi radio assumes that a collision has happened (this is called Collision Detection) and stops transmitting, since it knows that no data will be received by the destination WiFi radio.

We humans do a similar thing in a room full of people. When two people start talking at the same time, they are good at noticing that another person is talking and quickly stop talking. But the problem is how to restart the conversation. After a long pause it is common that both people start talking at the exact same time *again*. This can happen over and over and each person says "No, you" repeatedly to attempt to figure out how to get the conversation restarted. It can be quite comical at times.

The WiFi radios in two computers that send colliding packets are able to solve this problem much better than people can solve the problem. When the WiFi radios detect a collision or garbled transmission, they compute a random amount of time to wait before retrying the transmission. The rules for computing the random wait are set up to make sure the two colliding stations pick different amounts of time to wait before attempting to retransmit the packet.

The formal name for the listen, transmit, listen, and wait and retry if necessary is called "Carrier Sense Multiple Access with Collision Detection" or CSMA/CD.

It might sound a little chaotic to just "give it a try" and then "give it another try" if your transmission collides with another station's transmission. But in practice it works well. There is a whole category of link layers that use this basic pattern of listen, transmit, listen, and optionally retry. Wired Ethernet, cellular telephone data, and even Short Message Service (SMS/Texting) all use this "try then retry" approach.

3.3 Coordination in Other Link Layers

Sometimes when a link layer has many transmitting stations and needs to operate at near 100% efficiency for long periods of time, the design takes a different approach. In this approach, there is a "token" that indicates when each station is given the opportunity to transmit data. Stations cannot start a transmission unless they have the token. Instead of listening for "silence" and jumping in, they must wait for their turn to come around.

When a station receives the token and has a packet to send, it sends the packet. Once the packet has been sent, the station gives up the token and waits until the token comes back to it. If none of the stations have any data to send, the token is moved from one computer to the next computer as quickly as possible.

A group of people sitting around a meeting could communicate without ever interrupting each other by having a small ball that they pass around in a circle and only allowing the person who has the ball to speak. When you get the ball and have something to say you talk for a short period (transmit a packet of words) and then pass the ball on.

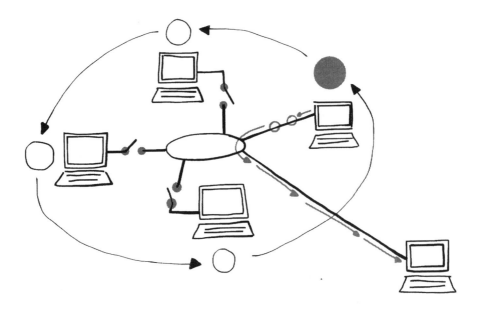

Figure 3.2: Communicating with a Token

The "try then retry" CSMA/CD approach works very well when there is no data or when low or moderate levels of data are being sent. But on a token-style network, if there is no data being sent and you want to send a packet, you still have to wait for a while before you receive the token and can start transmitting. When you finish your packet you have to wait until the token comes back before you can send the next packet. If you are the only station that wants to send data, you spend a good bit of time waiting for the token to come back to you after passing through all of the other stations.

The token approach is best suited when using a link medium such as as a satellite link or a undersea fiber optic link where it might take too long or be too costly to detect a collision. The CSMA/CD (listen-try) is best suited when the medium is inexpensive, shorter distance, and there are a lot of stations sharing the medium that only send data in short bursts. So that is why WiFi (and CSMA/CD) is so effective for providing network access in a coffee shop, home, or room in a school.

3.4 Summary

So now we have looked at the "lowest" layer in our four-layer architecture. And we have only taken a simple look at how the

Link layer works. There are many other details that must be designed into a link layer like connection distance, voltage, frequency, speed, and many others.

A key benefit of the layered architecture is that engineers who design and build Link layer technologies can ignore all of the issues that are handled by the layers above the Link layer. This allows them to focus on building the best possible solution to moving data across a single "hop". Modern-day link layers like WiFi, satellite, cable modems, Ethernet, and cellular technology are very well developed. Data moves so quickly and seamlessly that once we get our connection we rarely have to worry about the Link layer. It just works.

3.5 Glossary

base station: Another word for the first router that handles your packets as they are forwarded to the Internet.

broadcast: Sending a packet in a way that all the stations connected to a local area network will receive the packet.

gateway: A router that connects a local area network to a wider area network such as the Internet. Computers that want to send data outside the local network must send their packets to the gateway for forwarding.

MAC Address: An address that is assigned to a piece of network hardware when the device is manufactured.

token: A technique to allow many computers to share the same physical media without collisions. Each computer must wait until it has received the token before it can send data.

3.6 Questions

You can take this quiz online at http://www.net-intro.com/quiz/

1. When using a WiFi network to talk to the Internet, where does your computer send its packets?

   a) A gateway
   b) A satellite

c) A cell phone tower

d) The Internet Central Office

2. How is the link/physical address for a network device assigned?

a) By the cell tower

b) By the Internet Assignment Numbers Authority (IANA)

c) By the manufacturer of the link equipment

d) By the government

3. Which of these is a link address?

a) 0f:2a:b3:1f:b3:1a

b) 192.168.3.14

c) www.khanacademy.com

d) @drchuck

4. How does your computer find the gateway on a WiFi network?

a) It has a gateway address installed by the manufacturer

b) It broadcasts a request for the address of the gateway

c) It repeatedly sends a message to all possible gateway addresses until it finds one that works

d) The user must enter the gateway address by hand

5. When your computer wants to send data across WiFi, what is the first thing it must do?

a) Listen to see if other computers are sending data

b) Just start sending the data

c) Send a message to the gateway asking for permission to transmit

d) Wait until informed that it is your turn to transmit

6. What does a WiFi-connected workstation do when it tries to send data and senses a collision has happened?

a) Keep sending the message so part of the message makes it through

b) Wait until told by the gateway that the collision is over
c) Immediately restart transmitting the message at the beginning
d) Stop transmitting and wait a random amount of time before restarting

7. When a station wants to send data across a "token"-style network, what is the first thing it must do?

a) Listen to see if other computers are sending data
b) Just start sending the data
c) Send a message to the gateway asking for permission to transmit
d) Wait until informed that it is your turn to transmit

Chapter 4

Internetworking Layer (IP)

Now that we can move data across a single link, it's time to figure out how to move it across the country or around the world. To send data from your computer to any of a billion destinations, the data needs to move across multiple hops and across multiple networks. When you travel from your home to a distant destination, you might walk from your home to a bus stop, take a train to the city, take another train to the airport, take a plane to a different airport, take a taxi into the city, then take a train to a smaller town, a bus to an even smaller town, and finally walk from the bus stop to your hotel. A packet also needs to take multiple forms of transportation to reach its destination. For a packet taking its "trip" to another country, the "walk", "bus", "train", and "plane" can be thought of as different link layers like WiFi, Ethernet, fiber optic, and satellite.

At each point during the trip, you (or your packet) are being transported using a shared medium. There might be hundreds of other people on the same bus, train, or plane, but your trip is different from that of every other traveller because of the decisions that you make at the end of each of your "hops". For instance, when you arrive at a train station, you might get off one train, then walk through the station and select a particular outbound train to continue your journey. Travellers with different starting points and destinations make a different series of choices. All of the choices you make during your trip result in you following a series of links (or hops) along a route that takes you from your starting point to your destination.

As your packet travels from its starting point to its destination,

Figure 4.1: Travelling Packets

it also passes through a number of "stations" where a decision is made as to which output link your packet will be forwarded on. For packets, we call these places "routers". Like train stations, routers have many incoming and outgoing links. Some links may be fiber optic, others might be satellite, and still others might be wireless. The job of the router is to make sure packets move through the router and end up on the correct outbound link layer. A typical packet passes through from five to 20 routers as it moves from its source to its destination.

But unlike a train station where you need to look at displays to figure out the next train you need to take, the router looks at the destination address to decide which outbound link your packet needs to take. It is as if a train station employee met every single person getting off an inbound train, asked them where they were headed, and escorted them to their next train. If you were a packet, you would never have to look at another screen with a list of train departures and tracks!

The router is able to quickly determine the outbound link for your packet because every single packet is marked with its ultimate destination address. This is called the Internet Protocol Address, or IP Address for short. We carefully construct IP addresses to make the router's job of forwarding packets as efficient as possible.

4.1 Internet Protocol (IP) Addresses

In the previous section where we talked about Link layer addresses, we said that link addresses were assigned when the hardware was manufactured and stayed the same throughout the life of a computer. We cannot use link layer addresses to route packets across multiple networks because there is no relationship between a link layer address and the location where that computer is connected to the network. With portable computers and cell phones moving constantly, the system would need to track each individual computer as it moved from one location to another. And with billions of computers on the network, using the link layer address to make routing decisions would be slow and inefficient.

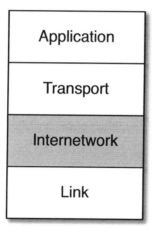

Figure 4.2: The Internetwork Layer

To make this easier, we assign another address to every computer based on where the computer is connected to the network. There are two different versions of IP addresses. The old (classic) IPv4 addresses consist of four numbers separated by dots like this, and look like this:

212.78.1.25

Each of the numbers can only be from 0 through 255. We have so many computers connected to the Internet now that we are running out of IPv4 addresses to assign to them. IPv6 address are longer and look like:

```
2001:0db8:85a3:0042:1000:8a2e:0370:7334
```

For this section we will focus on the classic IPv4 addresses, but all of the ideas apply equally to IPv4 and IPv6 addresses.

The most important thing about of IP addresses is that they can be broken into two parts.[1] The first part of the two-piece address is called the "Network Number". If we break out an IPv4 address into two parts, we might find the following:

```
Network Number: 212.78
Host Identifier: 1.25
```

The idea is that many computers can be connected via a single connection to the Internet. An entire college campus, school, or business could connect using a single network number, or only a few network numbers. In the example above, 65,536 computers could be connected to the network using the network number of "212.78". Since all of the computers appear to the rest of the Internet on a single connection, all packets with an IP address of:

```
212.78.*.*
```

can be routed to the same location.

By using this approach of a network number and a host identifier, routers no longer have to keep track of billions of individual computers. Instead, they need to keep track of perhaps a million or less different network numbers.

So when your packet arrives in a router and the router needs to decide which outbound link to send your packet to, the router does not have to look at the entire IP address. It only needs to look at the first part of the address to determine the best outbound link.

---

[1]There are many points where an IP address can be broken into "Network Number" and "Host Identifier" - for this example, we will just split the address in half.

4.2 How Routers Determine the Routes

While the idea of the collapsing many IP addresses into a single network number greatly reduces the number of individual end-points that a router must track to properly route packets, each router still needs a way to learn the path from itself to each of the network numbers it might encounter.

When a new core router is connected to the Internet, it does not know all the routes. It may know a few preconfigured routes, but to build a picture of how to route packets it must discover routes as it encounters packets. When a router encounters a packet that it does not already know how to route, it queries the routers that are its "neighbors". The neighboring routers that know how to route the network number send their data back to the request-ing router. Sometimes the neighboring routers need to ask their neighbors and so on until the route is actually found and sent back to the requesting router.

In the simplest case, a new core router can be connected to the Internet and slowly build a map of network numbers to outbound links so it can properly route packets based on the IP address for each incoming packet. We call this mapping of network numbers to outbound links the "routing table" for a particular router.

When the Internet is running normally, each router has a rela-tively complete routing table and rarely encounters a new net-work number. Once a router figures out the route to a new net-work number the first time it sees a packet destined for that net-work number, it does not need to rediscover the route for the network number unless something changes or goes wrong. This means that the router does a lookup on the first packet, but then it could route the next billion packets to that network number just by using the information it already has in its routing tables.

4.3 When Things Get Worse and Better

Sometimes the network has problems and a router must find a way to route data around the problems. A common problem is that one of the outbound links fails. Perhaps someone tripped over a wire and unplugged a fiber optic cable. At this point, the router has a bunch of network numbers that it wants to route out on a link that has failed. The recovery when a router loses an outbound link is surprisingly simple. The router discards all of the entries in its routing table that were being routed on that link. Then as more packets arrive for those network numbers, the router goes through the route discovery process again, this time asking all the neighboring routers except the ones that can no longer be contacted due to the broken link.

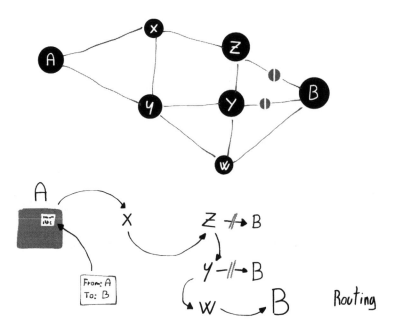

Figure 4.3: Dynamic Routing

Packets are routed more slowly for a while as routing tables are rebuilt that reflect the new network configuration, but after a while things are humming along nicely.

This is why it is important for there to always be at least two independent paths from a source network to a destination network in the core of the network. If there are always at least two possible independent routes, we say that a network is a "two-connected network". A two-connected network can recover from any single link outage. In places where there are a lot of network connections, like the east coast of the United States, the network could lose many links without ever becoming completely disconnected. But when you are at your home or school and have only one connection, if that connection goes down you are disconnected completely.

At some point the broken link is repaired or a new link is brought up, and the router wants to make best use of the new links. The router is always interested in improving its routing tables, and looks for opportunities to improve its routing tables in its spare time. When there is a lull in communication, a router will ask a neighboring router for all or part of its routing table. The router looks through the neighbor's tables and if it looks like the other router has a better route to a particular network number, it updates its network table to forward packets for that network number through the link to the router that has a better route.

With these approaches to outages and the exchange of routing table information, routers can quickly react to network outages and reroute packets from links that are down or slow to links that are up and/or faster. All the while, each router is talking to its neighboring routers to find ways to improve its own routing table. Even though there is no central source of the "best route" from any source to any destination, the routers are good at knowing the fastest path from a source to a destination nearly all the time. Routers are also good at detecting and dynamically routing packets around links that are slow or temporarily overloaded.

One of the side effects of the way routers discover the structure of the network is that the route your packets take from the source to the destination can change over time. You can even send one packet immediately followed by another packet and because of how the packets are routed, the second packet might arrive at the destination before the first packet. We don't ask the IP layer to worry about the order of the packets; it already has enough to worry about.

We pour our packets with source and destination IP addresses into the Internet much like we would send out a bunch of letters in the mail at the post office. The packets each find their way though the system and arrive at their destinations.

4.4 Determining Your Route

There is no place in the Internet that knows in advance the route your packets will take from your computer to a particular destination. Even the routers that participate in forwarding your packets across the Internet do not know the entire route your packet will take. They only know which link to send your packets to so they will get closer to their final destination.

But it turns out that most computers have a network diagnostic tool called "traceroute" (or "tracert", depending on the operating system) that allows you to trace the route between your computer and a destination computer. Given that the route between any two computers can change from one packet to another, when we "trace" a route, it is only a "pretty good guess" as to the actual route packets will take.

The traceroute command does not actually "trace" your packet at all. It takes advantage of a feature in the IP network protocol that was designed to avoid packets becoming "trapped" in the network and never reaching their destination. Before we take a look at traceroute, let's take a quick look at how a packet might get trapped in the network forever and how the IP protocol solves that problem.

Remember that the information in any single router is imperfect and is only an approximation of the best outbound link for a particular network number, and each router has no way of knowing what any other router will do. But what if we had three routers with routing table entries that formed an endless loop?

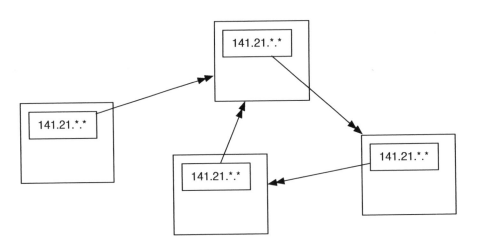

Figure 4.4: Routing Vortex

Each of the routers thinks it knows the best outbound link for IP addresses that start with "212.78". But somehow the routers are a little confused and their routing tables form a loop. If a packet with a prefix of "212.78" found its way into one of these routers, it would be routed around a circle of three links forever. There is no way out. As more packets arrived with the same prefix, they would just be added to the "infinite packet vortex". Pretty soon the links would be full of traffic going round and round, the routers would fill up with packets waiting to be sent, and all three routers would crash. This problem is worse than having someone trip over a fiber optic cable, since it can cause several routers to crash.

To solve this problem, the Internet Protocol designers added a number to each packet that is called the Time To Live (TTL). This number starts out with a value of about 30. Each time an IP packet is forwarded down a link, the router subtracts 1 from the TTL value. So if the packet takes 15 hops to cross the Internet, it will emerge on the far end with a TTL of 15.

But now let's look at how the TTL functions when there is a routing loop (or "packet vortex") for a particular network number. Since the packet keeps getting forwarded around the loop, eventually the TTL reaches zero. And when the TTL reaches zero, the router assumes that something is wrong and throws the packet away. This approach ensures that routing loops do not bring whole areas of the network down.

So that is a pretty cool bit of network protocol engineering. To detect and recover from routing loops, we just put a number in, subtract 1 from that number on each link, and when the number goes to zero throw the packet away.

It also turns out that when the router throws a packet away, it usually sends back a courtesy notification, something like, "Sorry I had to throw your packet away." The message includes the IP address of the router that threw the packet away.

Network loops are actually pretty rare, but we can use this notification that a packet was dropped to map the approximate route a packet takes through the network. The traceroute program sends packets in a tricky manner to get the routers that your packets pass through to send it back notifications. First, traceroute sends a packet with a TTL of 1. That packet gets to the first router and is discarded and your computer gets a notification from the first router. Then traceroute sends a packet with a TTL of 2. That packet makes it through the first router and is dropped by the second router, which sends you back a note about the discarded packet. Then traceroute sends a packet with a TTL of 3, and continues to increase the TTL until the packet makes it all the way to its destination.

With this approach, traceroute builds up an approximate path that your packets are taking across the network.

It took 14 hops to get from Ann Arbor, Michigan to Palo Alto, California. The packets passed through Kansas, Texas, Los Angeles, and Oakland. This might not be the best route between the two cities if you were driving a car or taking a train, but on that day

```
traceroute www.stanford.edu
traceroute to www5.stanford.edu (171.67.20.37), 64 hops max, 40 byte packets
 1  141.211.203.252 (141.211.203.252)  1.390 ms  0.534 ms  0.490 ms
 2  v-bin-seb.r-bin-seb.umnet.umich.edu (192.122.183.61)  0.591 ms  0.558 ms  0.570 ms
 3  v-bin-seb-i2-aa.merit-aa2.umnet.umich.edu (192.12.80.33)  6.610 ms  6.545 ms  6.654 ms
 4  192.122.183.30 (192.122.183.30)  7.919 ms  7.209 ms  7.122 ms
 5  so-4-3-0.0.rtr.kans.net.internet2.edu (64.57.28.36)  17.672 ms  17.836 ms  17.673 ms
 6  so-0-1-0.0.rtr.hous.net.internet2.edu (64.57.28.57)  31.800 ms  41.967 ms  31.787 ms
 7  so-3-0-0.0.rtr.losa.net.internet2.edu (64.57.28.44)  63.478 ms  63.704 ms  63.710 ms
 8  hpr-lax-hpr--i2-newnet.cenic.net (137.164.26.132)  63.093 ms  63.026 ms  63.384 ms
 9  svl-hpr--lax-hpr-10ge.cenic.net (137.164.25.13)  71.242 ms  71.542 ms  76.282 ms
10  oak-hpr--svl-hpr-10ge.cenic.net (137.164.25.9)  72.744 ms  72.243 ms  72.556 ms
11  hpr-stan-ge--oak-hpr.cenic.net (137.164.27.158)  73.763 ms  73.396 ms  73.665 ms
12  bbra-rtr.Stanford.EDU (171.64.1.134)  73.577 ms  73.682 ms  73.492 ms
13  * * *
14  www5.Stanford.EDU (171.67.20.37)  77.317 ms  77.128 ms  77.648 ms
```

Figure 4.5: Traceroute from Michigan to Stanford

for packets between the two cities this was the best route on the Internet.

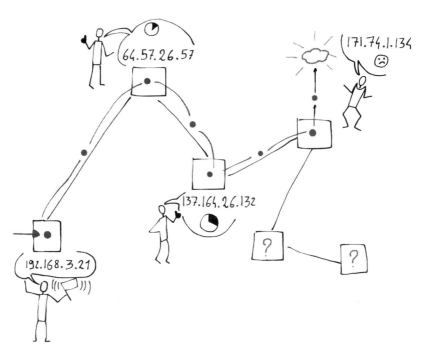

Figure 4.6: Notifications of Dropped Packets

You can also see how long it took the packets to make it from the source to each router, and then from the source to the destination. A millisecond (ms) is a 1/1000 of a second. So 77.317 ms is just under a tenth of a second. This network is pretty fast.

Sometimes a traceroute can take a little while, up to a minute or two. Not all routers will give you the "I discarded your packet" message. In the example above, the router at hop 13 threw our packet away without saying "I am sorry". Traceroute waits for the message and after a few seconds just gives up and increases the TTL value so it gets past the rude router.

If you run a traceroute for a connection that includes an undersea cable, you can see how fast data moves under the sea. Here is a traceroute between the University of Michigan and Peking University in China.

```
$ traceroute www.pku.edu.cn
traceroute to www.pku.edu.cn (162.105.129.104), 64 hops max, 40 byte packets
 1  141.211.203.252 (141.211.203.252)  1.228 ms  0.584 ms  0.592 ms
 2  v-bin-seb.r-bin-seb.umnet.umich.edu (192.122.183.61)  0.604 ms  0.565 ms  0.466 ms
 3  v-bin-seb-i2-aa.merit-aa2.umnet.umich.edu (192.12.80.33)  7.511 ms  6.641 ms  6.588 ms
 4  192.122.183.30 (192.122.183.30)  12.078 ms  6.989 ms  7.619 ms
 5  192.31.99.133 (192.31.99.133)  7.666 ms  8.953 ms  17.861 ms
 6  192.31.99.170 (192.31.99.170)  59.275 ms  59.273 ms  59.108 ms
 7  134.75.108.209 (134.75.108.209)  173.614 ms  173.552 ms  173.333 ms
 8  134.75.107.10 (134.75.107.10)  256.760 ms 134.75.107.18 (134.75.107.18)  256.574 ms
 9  202.112.53.17 (202.112.53.17)  256.761 ms  256.801 ms  256.688 ms
10  202.112.61.157 (202.112.61.157)  257.416 ms  257.960 ms  257.747 ms
11  202.112.53.194 (202.112.53.194)  256.827 ms  257.068 ms  256.962 ms
12  202.112.41.202 (202.112.41.202)  256.800 ms  257.053 ms  256.933 ms
```

Figure 4.7: Traceroute from Michigan to Peking University

You can see when the packet is encountering a long undersea cable in steps seven and eight. The time goes from less than 1/10 of a second to nearly 1/4 of a second. Even though 1/4 of a second is slower than 1/10 a second, it is pretty impressive when you consider that the packet is going nearly all of the way around the world in that 1/4 second.

The core of our IP network is remarkable. Most of the time we don't really care how hard the routers are working to make sure our packets move quickly from our computer to the various destinations around the world. Next we will move from looking at how the core of the network functions to how IP addresses are managed at the edges.

4.5 Getting an IP Address

Increasingly, computers are portable or mobile. We just pointed out how important it was for the IP layer to track large groups of computers using network numbers instead of tracking every single computer individually. But since these network numbers indicate a particular physical connection to the network, when we move a computer from one location to another, it will need a new IP address. Remember that the link layer address is set when a computer is manufactured and never changes throughout the life of the computer. If you close your laptop in one coffee shop and reopen it using your home WiFi, your computer will need a different IP address.

This ability for your computer to get a different IP address when it is moved from one network to another uses a protocol called "Dynamic Host Configuration Protocol" (or DHCP for short). DHCP is pretty simple. Going back to the Link layer section, recall the first thing your computer does at the link level is ask "Is there a base station on this network?" by sending a message to a special broadcast address. Once your computer is successfully connected at the link layer through that base station, it sends another broadcast message, this time asking "Is there a gateway connected to this network that can get me to the Internet? If there is, tell me your IP address and tell me what IP address I should use on this network".

When the gateway router replies, your computer is given a temporary IP address to use on that network (for instance, while you are at the coffee shop). After the router has not heard from your computer for a while, it decides you are gone and loans the IP address to another computer.

If this process of reusing a loaned IP address goes wrong, two computers end up on the same network with the same IP address. Perhaps you have seen a message on your computer to the effect of, "Another computer is using 192.168.0.5, we have stopped using this address". Your computer sees another computer with a link address other than its own using the IP address that your computer thinks is assigned to it.

But most of the time this dynamic IP address assignment (DHCP) works perfectly. You open your laptop and in a few seconds you are connected and can use the Internet. Then you close your laptop and go to a different location and are given a different IP address to use at that location.

In some operating systems, when a computer connects to a network, issues a DHCP request, and receives no answer, it decides to assign itself an IP address anyway. Often these self-assigned addresses start with "169. . . .". When your computer has one of these self-assigned IP addresses, it thinks it is connected to a network and has an IP address, but without a gateway, it has no possibility of getting packets routed across the local network and onto the Internet. The best that can be done is that a few computers can connect to a local network, find each other, and play

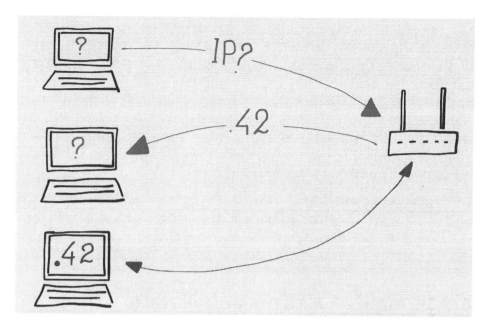

Figure 4.8: Getting an IP Address via DHCP

a networked game. There is not much else that can be done with these self-assigned IP addresses.

4.6 A Different Kind of Address Reuse

If you know how to find the IP address on your laptop, you can do a little experiment and look at the different IP addresses you get at different locations. If you made a list of the different addresses you received at the different locations, you might find that many of the locations give out addresses with a prefix of "192.168.". This seems to be a violation of the rule that the network number (IP address prefix) is tied to the place where the computer is connected to the Internet, but a different rule applies to addresses that start with "192.168." (The prefix "10." is also special).

Addresses that start with "192.168." are called "non-routable" addresses. This means that they will never be used as real addresses that will route data across the core of the network. They can be used within a single local network, but not used on the global network.

So then how is it that your computer gets an address like "192.168.0.5" on your home network and it works perfectly well on the overall Internet? This is because your home router/gateway/base station is doing something we call "Network Address Translation", or "NAT". The gateway has a single routable IP address that it is sharing across multiple workstations that are connected to the gateway. Your computer uses its non-routable address like "192.160.0.5" to send its packets, but as the packets move across the gateway, the gateway replaces the address with its actual routable address. When packets come back to your workstation, the router puts your workstation's non-routable address back into the returning packets.

This approach allows us to conserve the real routable addresses and use the same non-routable addresses over and over for workstations that move from one network to another.

4.7   Global IP Address Allocation

If you wanted to connect the network for a new organization to the Internet you would need to contact an Internet Service Provider and make a connection. Your ISP would give you a range of IP addresses (i.e., one or more network numbers) that you could allocate to the computers attached to your network. The ISP assigns you network numbers by giving you a portion of the network numbers they received from a higher-level Internet Service Provider.

At the top level of IP address allocations are five Regional Internet Registries (RIRs). Each of the five registries allocates IP addresses for a major geographic area. Between the five registries, every location in the world can be allocated a network number. The five registries are North America (ARIN), South and Central America (LACNIC), Europe (RIPE NCC), Asia-Pacific (APNIC) and Africa (AFRNIC).

When the classic IPv4 addresses like "212.78.1.25" were invented, only a few thousand computers were connected to the Internet. We never imagined then that someday we would have a billion computers on the Internet. But today with the expansion of the Internet and the "Internet of things" where smart cars, refrigerators, thermostats, and even lights will need IP addresses, we need to connect far more than a billion computers to the Internet. To make it possible to connect all these new computers to the Internet, engineers have designed a a new generation of the Internet Protocol called "IPv6". The 128-bit IPv6 addresses are much longer than the 32-bit IPv4 addresses.

The Regional Internet Registries (RIRs) are leading the transition from IPv4 to IPv6. The transition from IPv4 to IPv6 will take many years. During that time, both IPv4 and IPv6 must work seamlessly together.

4.8 Summary

The Internetworking Protocol layer extends our network from a single hop (Link layer) to a series of hops that result in packets quickly and efficiently being routed from your computer to a destination IP address and back to your computer. The IP layer is designed to react and route around network outages and maintain near-ideal routing paths for packets moving between billions of computers without any kind of central routing clearinghouse. Each router learns its position within the overall network, and by cooperating with its neighboring routers helps move packets effectively across the Internet.

The IP layer is not 100% reliable. Packets can be lost due to momentary outages or because the network is momentarily "confused" about the path that a packet needs to take across the network. Packets that your system sends later can find a quicker route through the network and arrive before packets that your system sent earlier.

It might seem tempting to design the IP layer so that it never loses packets and insures that packets arrive in order, but this would make it nearly impossible for the IP layer to handle the extreme complexities involved in connecting so many systems.

So instead of asking too much of the IP layer, we leave the problem of packet loss and packets that arrive out of order to our next layer up, the Transport layer.

4.9 Glossary

core router: A router that is forwarding traffic within the core of the Internet.

DHCP: Dynamic Host Configuration Protocol. DHCP is how a portable computer gets an IP address when it is moved to a new location.

edge router: A router which provides a connection between a local network and the Internet. Equivalent to "gateway".

Host Identifier: The portion of an IP address that is used to identify a computer within a local area network.

IP Address: A globally assigned address that is assigned to a computer so that it can communicate with other computers that have IP addresses and are connected to the Internet. To simplify routing in the core of the Internet IP addresses are broken into Network Numbers and Host Identifiers. An example IP address might be "212.78.1.25".

NAT: Network Address Translation. This technique allows a single global IP address to be shared by many computers on a single local area network.

Network Number: The portion of an IP address that is used to identify which local network the computer is connected to.

packet vortex: An error situation where a packet gets into an infinite loop because of errors in routing tables.

RIR: Regional Internet Registry. The five RIRs roughly correspond to the continents of the world and allocate IP address for the major geographical areas of the world.

routing tables: Information maintained by each router that keeps track of which outbound link should be used for each network number.

Time To Live (TTL): A number that is stored in every packet that is reduced by one as the packet passes through each router. When the TTL reaches zero, the packet is discarded.

traceroute: A command that is available on many Linux/UNIX systems that attempts to map the path taken by a packet as it moves from its source to its destination. May be called "tracert" on Windows systems.

two-connected network: A situation where there is at least two possible paths between any pair of nodes in a network. A two-connected network can lose any single link without losing overall connectivity.

4.10 Questions

You can take this quiz online at http://www.net-intro.com/quiz/

1. What is the goal of the Internetworking layer?

   a) Move packets across multiple hops from a source to destination computer
   b) Move packets across a single physical connection
   c) Deal with web server failover
   d) Deal with encryption of sensitive data

2. How many different physical links does a typical packet cross from its source to its destination on the Internet?

   a) 1
   b) 4
   c) 15
   d) 255

3. Which of these is an IP address?

   a) 0f:2a:b3:1f:b3:1a
   b) 192.168.3.14
   c) www.khanacademy.com
   d) @drchuck

4. Why is it necessary to move from IPv4 to IPv6?

   a) Because IPv6 has smaller routing tables
   b) Because IPv6 reduces the number of hops a packet must go across
   c) Because we are running out of IPv4 addresses
   d) Because IPv6 addresses are chosen by network hardware manufacturers

5. What is a network number?

   a) A group of IP addresses with the same prefix
   b) The GPS coordinates of a particular LAN
   c) The number of hops it takes for a packet to cross the network
   d) The overall delay packets experience crossing the network

6. How many computers can have addresses within network number "218.78"?

a) 650
b) 6500
c) 65000
d) 650000

7. How do routers determine the path taken by a packet across the Internet?

a) The routes are controlled by the IRG (Internet Routing Group)
b) Each router looks at a packet and forwards it based on its best guess as to the correct outbound link
c) Each router sends all packets on every outbound link (flooding algorithm)
d) Each router holds on to a packet until a packet comes in from the destination computer

8. What is a routing table?

a) A list of IP addresses mapped to link addresses
b) A list of IP addresses mapped to GPS coordinates
c) A list of network numbers mapped to GPS coordinates
d) A list of network numbers mapped to outbound links from the router

9. How does a newly connected router fill its routing tables?

a) By consulting the IANA (Internet Assigned Numbers Authority)
b) By downloading the routing RFC (Request for Comments)
c) By contacting the Internet Engineering Task Force (IETF)
d) By asking neighboring routers how they route packets

10. What does a router do when a physical link goes down?

a) Throws away all of the routing table entries for that link
b) Consults the Internet Map (IMAP) service
c) Does a Domain Name (DNS) looking for the IP address
d) Sends all the packets for that link back to the source computer

11. Why is it good to have at least a "two-connected" network?

a) Because routing tables are much smaller
b) Because it removes the need for network numbers
c) Because it supports more IPv4 addresses
d) Because it continues to function even when a single link goes down

12. Do all packets from a message take the same route across the Internet?

a) Yes
b) No

13. How do routers discover new routes and improve their routing tables?

a) Each day at midnight they download a new Internet map from IMAP
b) They periodically ask neighboring routers for their network tables
c) They randomly discard packets to trigger error-correction code within the Internet
d) They are given transmission speed data by destination computers

14. What is the purpose of the "Time to Live" field in a packet?

a) To make sure that packets do not end up in an "infinite loop"
b) To track how many minutes it takes for a packet to get through the network
c) To maintain a mapping between network numbers and GPS coordinates
d) To tell the router the correct output link for a particular packet

15. How does the "traceroute" command work?

a) It sends a series of packets with low TTL values so it can get a picture of where the packets get dropped
b) It loads a network route from the Internet Map (IMAP)
c) It contacts a Domain Name Server to get the route for a particular network number

  d) It asks routers to append route information to a packet as it is routed from source to destination

16. About how long does it take for a packet to cross the Pacific Ocean via an undersea fiber optic cable?

  a) 0.0025 Seconds
  b) 0.025 Seconds
  c) 0.250 Seconds
  d) 2.5 Seconds

17. On a WiFi network, how does a computer get an Internetworking (IP) address?

  a) Using the DHCP protocol
  b) Using the DNS protocol
  c) Using the HTTP protocol
  d) Using the IMAP protocol

18. What is Network Address Translation (NAT)?

  a) It looks up the IP address associated with text names like "www.dr-chuck.com"
  b) It allows IPv6 traffic to go across IPv4 networks
  c) It looks up the best outbound link for a particular router and network number
  d) It reuses special network numbers like "192.168" across multiple network gateways at multiple locations

19. How are IP addresses and network numbers managed globally?

  a) There are five top-level registries that manage network numbers in five geographic areas
  b) IP addresses are assigned worldwide randomly in a lottery
  c) IP addresses are assigned by network equipment manufacturers
  d) IP addresses are based on GPS coordinates

20. How much larger are IPv6 addresses than IPv4 addresses?

  a) They are the same size

b) IPv6 addresses are 50% larger than IPv4 addresses

c) IPv6 addresses are twice as large as IPv4 addresses

d) IPv6 addresses are 10 times larger than IPv4 addresses

21. What does it mean when your computer receives an IP address that starts with "169.."?

a) Your connection to the Internet supports the Multicast protocol

b) The gateway is mapping your local address to a global address using NAT

c) There was no gateway available to forward your packets to the Internet

d) The gateway for this network is a low-speed gateway with a small window size

22. If you were starting an Internet Service Provider in Poland, which Regional Internet Registry (RIR) would assign you a block of IP addresses.

a) ARIN

b) LACNIC

c) RIPE NCC

d) APNIC

e) AFRNIC

f) United Nations

Chapter 5

The Domain Name System

The Domain Name System lets you access websites by their domain name like (www.khanacademy.org), so you don't have to keep a list of numeric Internet Protocol (IP) addresses like "212.78.1.25". IP address are determined by *where* your computer connects to the Internet. When you have a portable computer and you move from one location to another, you get a new IP address at each new location. Since no one connects to your portable computer, it does not matter if your IP address changes from time to time. But since so many people connect to a web server, it would be inconvenient if the server moved to a new location and needed to change its IP address.

When your computer makes a connection to a system using a domain name address, the first thing your computer does is look up the IP address that corresponds to the domain name. Then your computer makes the connection using the IP address.

Adding the separate step of looking up the IP address for a DNS address also makes it easier to move a server from one location to another. The server is given a new IP address and the entry for the domain address is updated. Once the DNS entry is updated, new requests for the domain name are given the new IP address. Since end users access most servers using domain names and never see the IP address, a server can be moved to a new network connection without affecting the end user's ability to access the server.

5.1 Allocating Domain Names

If you recall from the previous section, IP addresses are allocated based on where you connect a new network to the Internet. Domain names are allocated based on organizations that "own" the domain name. At the top of the domain name hierarchy is an organization called the International Corporation for Assigned Network Names (ICANN). ICANN chooses the top-level domains (TLDs) like .com, .edu, and .org and assigns those to other organizations to manage. Recently a new set of TLDs like .club and .help have been made available.

ICANN also assigns two-letter country code top-level domain names like .us, .za, .nl, and .jp to countries around the world We call these Country-Code Top-Level Domain Names (ccTLDs). Countries often add second-level TLDs, like .co.uk for commercial organizations within the UK. Policies for applying for domain names with any particular ccTLD vary widely from one country to another.

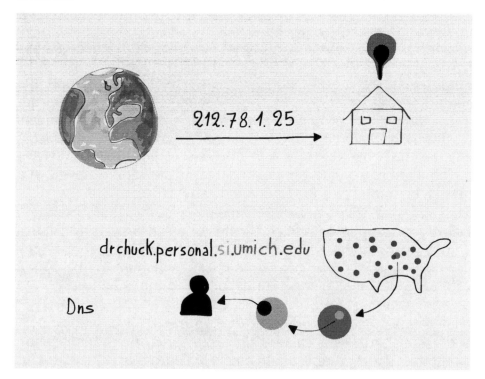

Figure 5.1: Domain Names

Once a domain name is assigned to an organization, the controlling organization is allowed to assign subdomains within the domain. As an example, the .edu top-level domain is assigned to the Educause organization. Educause assigns domains like umich.edu to higher education institutions. Once the University of Michigan is given control of umich.edu, it can make its own choices for subdomains within its new domain. Domains ending in .com and .org can be purchased by individuals. The individual owners of those domains are allowed to manage their domain and create subdomains under it for their own use or use by others.

5.2 Reading Domain Names

When we look at an IP address like "212.78.1.25", the left prefix is the "Network Number", so in a sense we read IP addresses from left to right, where the left part of the IP address is the most general part of the address and right part of the address is most specific:

```
212.78.1.25
Broad ----> Narrow
```

For domain names, we read from right to left:

```
drchuck.personal.si.umich.edu
Narrow          <---        Broad
```

The most general part of this domain name is ".edu", which means higher education institutions. The subdomain "umich.edu" is a particular higher education institution.

5.3 Summary

While the Domain Name System is not one of our four layers in the model, it is an important part of making the Internet easier to use. Domain names allow end users to use symbolic names for servers instead of numeric Internet Protocol addresses. By adding a service that maps domain names to IP addresses, we can move servers from one Internet connection to another connection without requiring users to manually change their configurations to connect to a server.

If you would like to purchase a domain name for yourself or your company, you can choose from any number of domain name registrars.

5.4   Glossary

DNS: Domain Name System. A system of protocols and servers that allow networked applications to look up domain names and retrieve the corresponding IP address for the domain name.

domain name: A name that is assigned within a top-level domain. For example, khanacademy.org is a domain that is assigned within the ".org" top-level domain.

ICANN: International Corporation for Assigned Network Names. Assigns and manages the top-level domains for the Internet.

registrar: A company that can register, sell, and host domain names.

subdomain: A name that is created "below" a domain name.   For example, "umich.edu" is a domain name and both "www.umich.edu" and "mail.umich.edu" are subdomains within "umich.edu".

TLD: Top Level Domain. The leftmost portion of the domain name. Example TLDs include ".com", ".org", and ".ru". Recently, new top-level domains like ".club" and ".help" were added.

5.5   Questions

You can take this quiz online at http://www.net-intro.com/quiz/

1. What does the Domain Name System accomplish?

   a) It allows network-connected computers to use a textual name for a computer and look up its IP address
   b) It keeps track of the GPS coordinates of all servers
   c) It allows Regional Internet Registries (RIRs) to manage IP addresses on the various continents
   d) It assigns different IP addresses to portable computers as they move from one WiFi to another

2. What organization assigns top-level domains like ".com", ".org", and ".club"?

   a) IANA - Internet Assigned Numbers Authority
   b) IETF - Internet Engineering Task Force

c) ICANN - International Corporation for Assigned Network Names
d) IMAP - Internet Mapping Authorization Prototol

3. Which of these is a domain address?

a) 0f:2a:b3:1f:b3:1a
b) 192.168.3.14
c) www.khanacademy.org
d) @drchuck

4. Which of these is *not* something a domain owner can do with their domain?

a) Create subdomains
b) Sell subdomains
c) Create new top-level domains
d) Assign an IP address to the domain or subdomain

Chapter 6

Transport Layer

The next layer up from the Internetworking layer is the Transport layer. A key element of the Internetworking layer is that it does not attempt to guarantee delivery of any particular packet. The Internetworking layer is nearly perfect, but sometimes packets can be lost or misrouted.

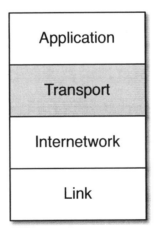

Figure 6.1: The Transport Layer

But users of the network want to reliably send entire files or messages across the Internet. A network is not much good to us if all it can do is send packets that are received most of the time. For the network to be useful, all of the packets need to be reassembled into the right order to reconstruct the message on the receiving system. The network must also deal with packets that arrive out of order or never arrive at all. The Transport layer is where we handle reliability and message reconstruction on the destination computer.

Just like the IP layer, the Transport layer adds a small amount of data to each packet to help solve the problems of packet reassembly and retransmission.

6.1 Packet Headers

If you were to look at a packet going across one of many links between its source and destination computers, you would see a link header, an IP header, and a Transport Control Protocol (TCP) header, along with the actual data in the packet.

Link Header	IP Header	TCP Header	Data Packet
From I To	From I To I TTL	Port I Offset	....

Figure 6.2: Headers and Data

The link header is removed when the packet is received on one link and a new link header is added when the packet is sent out on the next link on its journey. The IP and TCP headers stay with a packet as it is going across each link in its journey. Remember that a packet may go across several types of link layers as it is routed through the Internet.

The IP header holds the source and destination Internet Protocol (IP) addresses as well as the Time to Live (TTL) for the packet. The IP header is set on the source computer and is unchanged (other than the TTL) as the packet moves through the various routers on its journey.

The TCP headers indicate where the data in each packet belongs. As the source computer breaks the message or file into packets, it keeps track of the position of each packet relative to the beginning of the message or file and places the offset in each packet that is created and sent.

6.2 Packet Reassembly and Retransmission

As the destination computer receives the packets, it looks at the offset position from the beginning of the message so it can put the packet into the proper place in the reassembled message. Simply by making sure to put the packet data at the correct position relative to the beginning of the message, the Transport layer easily handles packets that arrive out of order. If it receives a packet further down a message, it places that packet in a buffer, keeping track of the fact that there is now a gap in the message that is being reconstructed. When the earlier packet arrives a moment later, it fits perfectly into the gap in the reassembled data.

To avoid overwhelming the network, the Transport layer in the sending computer only sends a certain amount of data before waiting for an acknowledgement from the Transport layer on the destination computer that the packets were received. The amount of data that the sending computer will send before pausing to wait for an acknowledgment is called the "window size".

The sending computer keeps track of how quickly it starts to receive acknowledgements from the receiving computer. If the acknowledgments come back quickly, the sending computer increases its window size, but if the acknowledgments come back slowly, the sending computer transmits less data. By adjusting the window size, transmitting computers can send large amounts of data quickly over fast connections that have light loads. When sending data over slow or heavily loaded links, they can send the data in a way that does not overwhelm the network.

If a packet is lost, it will never arrive at the destination computer and so the destination computer will never send an acknowledgment for that data. Because the sending computer does not receive an acknowledgment, it quickly reaches the point where it has sent enough unacknowledged data to fill up the window and stops sending new packets.

At this point, both computers are waiting. The sending computer is waiting for an acknowledgement for a lost packet that will never come and the receiving computer is waiting for a lost packet that will never come. To make sure that the computers do not wait forever, the destination computer keeps track of the amount of time since it received the last packet of data. At some point, the receiving computer decides too much time has passed and sends a packet to the sending computer indicating where in the stream the receiving computer has last received data. When the sending computer receives this message, it "backs up" and resends data from the last position that the receiving computer had successfully received.

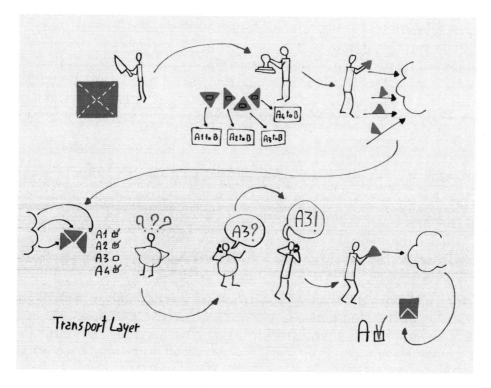

Figure 6.3: Waiting for a Lost Packet

The combination of the receiving computer acknowledging received data, not allowing the transmitting computer to get too far ahead (window size), and the receiving computer requesting the sending computer to "back up and restart" when it appears that data has been lost creates a relatively simple method to reliably send large messages or files across a network.

While the Transport layer is sending a stream of data, it continuously monitors how quickly it receives acknowledgements and dynamically adjusts its window size. This ensures that data is sent rapidly when the connection between two computers is fast and much more slowly when the connection has slow links or a heavy load.

6.3 The Transport Layer In Operation

One of the key elements of the Transport layer is that the sending computer must hold on to all of the data it is sending until the data has been acknowledged. Once the receiving computer acknowledges the data, the sending computer can discard the sent data. We can look at this graphically when a message is broken into many packets. Here, the first ten packets of the message have been sent and acknowledged by the destination computer ('a'). The sending computer has sent six more packets ('S'), and then stopped because it reached its window size.

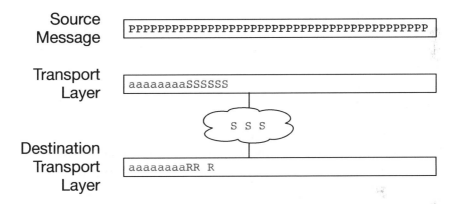

Figure 6.4: Buffering in the Transport Layer

There are three packets that have been sent but not yet received ("S"). Since there are many hops in the network, it is very common for more than one packet to be enroute in the network at the same time.

The Transport layer on the receiving computer has received and acknowledged ten packets and delivered them to the receiving application ('a').[1] The Transport layer on the destination computer has received more three packets ('R'), but one packet is out of order. Receiving a packet out of order is not a cause for concern if the missing packet arrives in a reasonably short amount of time. As long as all the packets are received, the receiving Transport layer will reconstruct the message, fitting the packets together like puzzle pieces, and deliver them to the receiving application.

---

[1]We talk about the Application layer in later material.

6.4   Application Clients and Servers

The purpose of the Transport layer is to provide reliable connections between networked applications so those applications can send and receive streams of data. For an application, this is as simple as asking the Transport layer to make a connection to an application running on a remote host. We call the application that initiates the connection on the local computer the "client" and the application that responds to the connection request the "server". We call the combination of the two networked applications at the ends of the connection a "client/server" application because the two pieces of the application must work together.

A lot of engineering has gone into the lower three layers of our architecture to make it easy to open a connection to a remote computer and then send and receive data over that connection.

6.5   Server Applications and Ports

When a client application wants to make a connection to a remote computer, it is important that the connection is made to the correct server application on that remote computer. A remote computer might have any number of different server applications running at the same time. Example server applications would include:

- Web Server
- Video Server
- Mail Server

For instance, a web client (a browser) needs to connect to the web server running on the remote computer. So a client application not only needs to know which remote computer to connect to, it also needs to choose a particular application to interact with on that remote computer.

We use a concept called "ports" to allow a client application to choose which server application it wants to interact with. Ports are like telephone extensions. All of the extensions have the same phone number (IP Address) but each extension (server application) has a different extension number (port number).

When a server application starts up, it "listens" for incoming connections on the specified port. Once the server application has

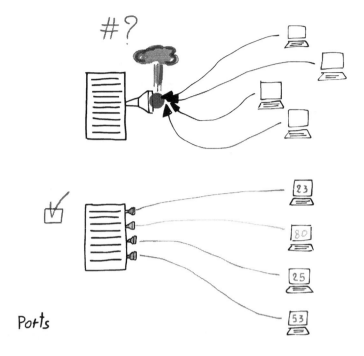

Figure 6.5: TCP Ports

registered that it is ready to receive incoming connections, it waits until the first connection is made.

So that client applications know which port to connect to, there is a list of well-known default ports for various server applications:

- Telnet (23) - Login
- SSH (22) - Secure Login
- HTTP (80) - World Wide Web
- HTTPS (443) - Secure Web
- SMTP (25) (Incoming Mail)
- IMAP (143/220/993) - Mail Retrieval
- POP (109/110) - Mail Retrieval
- DNS (53) - Domain Name Resolution
- FTP (21) - File Transfer

These are the normal ports for these applications. Sometimes servers will make applications available at non-standard ports. If you are doing web development, you may run a web server at a standard port like 3000, 8080, or 8888. If you see a URL like:

```
http://testing.example.com:8080/login
```

the "8080" indicates that your browser is to use the web protocols to interact with the server, but connect to port 8080 instead of the default port 80.

6.6   Summary

In a sense, the purpose of the Transport layer is to compensate for the fact that the Link and Internetworking layers might lose data.   When the two lower layers lose or reroute packets, the Transport layer works to reassemble and/or retransmit that data. The existence of the Transport layer makes it possible for the two lower layers to ignore retransmission and rate-limiting issues.

Part of the goal of a layered architecture is to break an overly complex problem into smaller subproblems. Each layer focuses on solving part of the overall problem and assumes that the other layers solve the problems they are supposed to solve.

6.7   Glossary

acknowledgement: When the receiving computer sends a no-tification back to the source computer indicating that data has been received.

buffering: Temporarily holding on to data that has been sent or received until the computer is sure the data is no longer needed.

listen: When a server application is started and ready to accept incoming connections from client applications.

port: A way to allow many different server applications to be waiting for incoming connections on a single computer.   Each application listens on a different port. Client applications make connections to well-known port numbers to make sure they are talking to the correct server application.

6.8   Questions

You can take this quiz online at http://www.net-intro.com/quiz/

   1. What is the primary problem the Transport (TCP) layer is sup-posed to solve?

a) Move packets across multiple hops from a source to destination computer
b) Move packets across a single physical connection
c) Deal with lost and out-of-order packets
d) Deal with encryption of sensitive data

2. What is in the TCP header?

a) Physical address
b) IP Address and Time to Live
c) Port number and offset
d) Which document is being requested

3. Why is "window size" important for the proper functioning of the network?

a) Because packets that are too large will clog fiber optic connections
b) It prevents a fast computer from sending too much data on a slow connection
c) It limits the number of hops a packet can take before it is dropped
d) It determines what part of an IP address is the network number

4. What happens when a sending computer receives an acknowledgement from the receiving computer?

a) The sending computer resends the data to make sure it was transmitted accurately.
b) The sending computer sends more data up to the window size
c) The sending computer sends an "acknowledgment for the acknowledgment"
d) The sending computer sends the acknowledgement to the Internet Map (IMAP)

5. Which of these detects and takes action when packets are lost?

a) Sending computer
b) Network gateway

   c) Core Internet routers
   d) Receiving computer

6. Which of these retains data packets so they can be retransmitted if a packets lost?

   a) Sending computer
   b) Network gateway
   c) Core Internet routers
   d) Receiving computer

7. Which of these is most similar to a TCP port?

   a) Train station
   b) Undersea network cable
   c) Apartment number
   d) Sculpture garden

8. Which half of the client/server application must start first?

   a) Client
   b) Server

9. What is the port number for the Domain Name System?

   a) 22
   b) 80
   c) 53
   d) 143

10. What is the port number for the IMAP mail retrieval protocol?

   a) 22
   b) 80
   c) 53
   d) 143

Chapter 7

Application Layer

We have been working from the bottom to the top of our four-layer TCP/IP network model and we are finally at the top. The Application layer is where the networked software like web browsers, mail programs, video players, or networked video players operate. We as users interact with these applications and the applications interact with the network on our behalf.

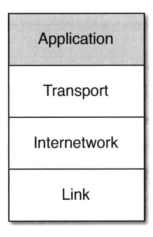

Figure 7.1: The Application Layer

7.1 Client and Server Applications

It is important to remember that two parts are required for a networked application to function. The architecture for a networked application is called "client/server". The server portion of the application runs somewhere on the Internet and has the information that users want to view or interact with. The client portion of the application makes connections to the server application, retrieves information, and shows it to the user. These applications use the Transport layer on each of their computers to exchange data.

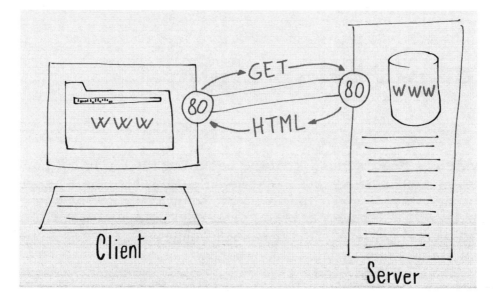

Figure 7.2: Client/Server Applications

To browse a web address like www.khanacademy.org, you must have a web application running on your computer. When you type an address into your web browser, it connects to the appropriate web server, retrieves pages for you to view, and then shows you the pages.

The web browser on your computer sends a request to connect to www.khanacademy.org. Your computer looks up the domain name to find the corresponding IP address for the server and makes a transport connection to that IP address, then begins to request data from the server over that network connection. When the data is received, the web browser shows it to you. Sometimes web browsers display a small animated icon to let you know that the data is being retrieved across the network.

On the other end of the connection is another application called a "web server". The web server program is always up and waiting for incoming connections. So when you want to see a web page, you are connecting to a server application that is already running and waiting for your connection.

In a sense, the Transport, Internetwork, and Link layers, along with the Domain Name System, are like a telephone network for networked applications. They "dial up" different server applications on the network and have "conversations" with those applications to exchange data.

7.2 Application Layer Protocols

Just like people talking on telephones, each pair of network applications needs a set of rules that govern the conversation. In most cultures, when your phone rings and you pick up the phone you say "Hello". Normally the person who made the call (the client person) is silent until the person who picked up the phone (the server person) says "Hello". If you have ever called someone who does not follow this simple rule, it can be quite confusing. You probably would assume that the connection was not working, hang up, and retry the call.

A set of rules that govern how we communicate is called a "protocol". The definition of the word protocol is "a rule which describes how an activity should be performed, especially in the field of diplomacy." The idea is that in formal situations, we should behave according to a precise set of rules. We use this word to describe networked applications, because without precise rules, applications have no way to establish and manage a conversation. Computers like precision.

There are many different networked applications and it is important that each networked application have a well-documented protocol so that all servers and clients can interoperate. Some of these protocols are intricate and complex.

The protocol that describes how a web browser communicates with a web server is described in a number of large documents starting with this one:

https://tools.ietf.org/html/rfc7230

The formal name of the protocol between web clients and web servers is the "HyperText Transport Protocol", or HTTP for short. When you put "http:" or "https:" on the beginning of a URL that you type into the browser, you are indicating that you would like to retrieve a document using the HTTP protocol.

If you were to read the above document, and go to section 5.3.2 on page 41, you find the exact text of what a web client is supposed to send to a web server:

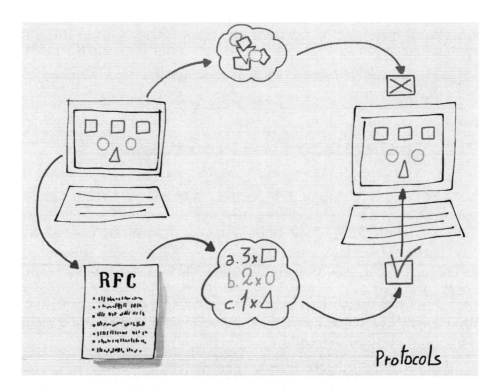

Figure 7.3: Application Protocols

GET http://www.example.org/pub/WWW/TheProject.html HTTP/1.1

One of the reasons that HTTP is so successful is that it is relatively simple compared to most client/server protocols. Even though the basic use of HTTP is relatively simple, there is a lot of detail that allows web clients and servers communicate efficiently and transfer a wide range of information and data. Six different documents describe the HTTP protocol, in a total of 305 pages. That might seem like a lot of detail, but the key in designing protocols is to think through all possible uses of the protocol and describe each scenario carefully.

7.3   Exploring the HTTP Protocol

In this section we will manually exercise the HTTP protocol by pretending to be a web browser and sending HTTP commands to a web server to retrieve data. To play with the HTTP protocol, we will use one of the earliest Internet applications ever built.

The "telnet" application was first developed in 1968, and was developed according to one of the earliest standards for the Internet:

https://tools.ietf.org/html/rfc15

This standard is only five pages long and at this point, you probably can easily read and understand most of what is in the document. The telnet client application is so old that it is effectively a dinosaur, as it comes from "prehistoric" times in terms of the age of the Internet. The Internet was created in 1985 by the NSFNet project and the precursor to the NSFNet called the ARPANET was brought up in 1969. Telnet was designed and built even before the first TCP/IP network was in production.

Interestingly, the telnet application is still present in most modern operating systems. You can access telnet from the terminal (command line) in Macintosh and Linux. The telnet application was also present in Windows 95 through Windows XP, but is not included in later versions of Windows. If you have a later version of Windows, you can download and install a telnet client to do the examples in this section.

Telnet is a simple application. Run telnet from the command line (or terminal) and type the following command:

```
telnet www.dr-chuck.com 80
```

The first parameter is a domain name (an IP address would work here as well) and a port to connect to on that host. We use the port to indicate which application server we would like to connect to. Port 80 is where we typically expect to find an HTTP (web) server application on a host. If there is no web server listening on port 80, our connection will time out and fail. But if there is a web server, we will be connected to that web server and whatever we type on our keyboard will be sent directly to the server. At this point, we need to know the HTTP protocol and type the commands precisely as expected. If we don't know the protocol, the web server will not be too friendly. Here is an example of things not going well:

```
telnet www.dr-chuck.com 80
Trying 198.251.66.43...
Connected to www.dr-chuck.com.
Escape character is '^]'.
HELP
<!DOCTYPE HTML PUBLIC "-//IETF//DTD HTML 2.0//EN">
```

```
<html><head>
<title>501 Method Not Implemented</title>
...
</body></html>
Connection closed by foreign host.
```

We type "telnet" in the terminal requesting a connection to port 80 (the web server) on the host www.dr-chuck.com. You can see as our transport layer is looking up the domain name, finding that the actual address is "198.251.66.43", and then making a successful connection to that server. Once we are connected, the server waits for us to type a command followed by the enter or return key. Since we don't know the protocol, we type "HELP" and enter. The server is not pleased, gives us an error message, and then closes the connection. We do not get a second chance. If we do not know the protocol, the web server does not want to talk to us.

But let's go back and read section 5.3.2 of the RFC-7230 document and try again to request a document using the correct syntax:

```
telnet www.dr-chuck.com 80
Trying 198.251.66.43...
Connected to www.dr-chuck.com.
Escape character is '^]'.
GET http://www.dr-chuck.com/page1.htm HTTP/1.0

HTTP/1.1 200 OK
Last-Modified: Sun, 19 Jan 2014 14:25:43 GMT
Content-Length: 131
Content-Type: text/html

<h1>The First Page</h1>
<p>
If you like, you can switch to the
<a href="http://www.dr-chuck.com/page2.htm">
Second Page</a>.
</p>
Connection closed by foreign host.
```

We make the connection to the web browser again using telnet, then we send a GET command that indicates which document we want to retrieve. We use version 1.0 of the HTTP protocol because

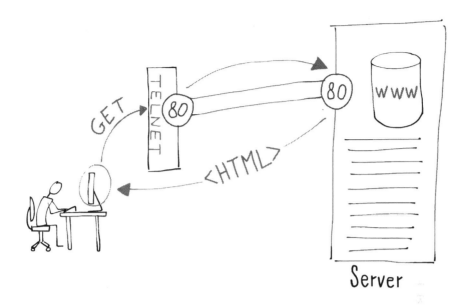

Figure 7.4: Hacking HTTP By Hand

it is simpler than HTTP 1.1. Then we send a blank line by pressing "return" or "enter" to indicate that we are done with our request.

Since we have sent the proper request, the host responds with a series of headers describing the document, followed by a blank line, then it sends the actual document.

The headers communicate metadata (data about data) about the document that we have asked to retrieve. For example, the first line contains a status code.

In this example, the status code of "200" means that things went well. A status code of "404" in the first line of the headers indicates that the requested document was not found. A status code of "301" indicates that the document has moved to a new location.

The status codes for HTTP are grouped into ranges: 2XX codes indicate success, 3XX codes are for redirecting, 4XX codes indicate that the client application did something wrong, and 5xx codes indicate that the server did something wrong.

This is a HyperText Markup Language (HTML) document, so it is marked up with tags like <h1> and <p>. When your browser receives the document in HTML format, it looks at the markup in the document, interprets it, and presents you a formatted version of the document.

7.4   The IMAP Protocol for Retrieving Mail

The HTTP protocol is only one of many client/server application protocols used on the Internet. Another common protocol is used so that a mail application running on your computer can retrieve mail from a central server. Since your personal computer might not be turned on at all times, when mail is sent to you it is sent to a server and stored on that server until you turn on your computer and retrieve any new email.

Like many application standards, the Internet Message Access Protocol (IMAP) is described in a series of Request For Comment (RFC) documents starting with this RFC:

```
https://tools.ietf.org/html/rfc3501
```

IMAP is a more complicated protocol than the web protocol, so we won't be able to use the telnet command to fake the protocol. But if you were going to develop a mail reading application, you could carefully read this document and develop code to have a successful conversation with a standards-compliant IMAP server. Here is a simple example from section 6.3.1 of the above document showing what the client (C:) sends and how the server (S:) responds:

```
C: A142 SELECT INBOX
S: * 172 EXISTS
S: * 1 RECENT
S: * OK [UNSEEN 12] Message 12 is first unseen
S: * OK [UIDVALIDITY 3857529045] UIDs valid
S: * OK [UIDNEXT 4392] Predicted next UID
S: * FLAGS (\Answered \Flagged \Deleted \Seen \Draft)
S: * OK [PERMANENTFLAGS (\Deleted \Seen \*)] Limited
S: A142 OK [READ-WRITE] SELECT completed
```

The messages that are sent by the client and server are not designed to be viewed by an end user so they are not particularly descriptive. These messages are precisely formatted and are sent in a precise order so that they can be generated and read by networked computer applications on each end of the connection.

7.5   Flow Control

When we looked at the Transport layer, we talked about the "window size", which was the amount of data that the Transport layer on the sending computer will send before pausing to wait for an acknowledgement.

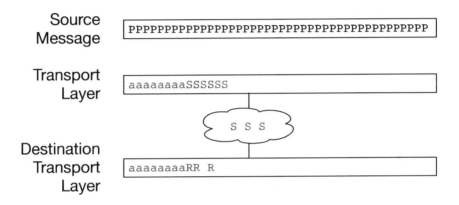

Figure 7.5: Buffering in the Transport Layer

In this figure, we see a message broken into packets, with some of the packets sent and acknowledged. Six packets have been sent but not yet acknowledged and the sending Transport layer has reached the limit of the transmit window, so it is pausing until it receives an acknowledgement from the receiving computer's Transport layer. The receiving computer has received three packets, one of which is out of order.

When we were looking at this example before from the point of view of the Transport layer, we ignored where the packets to be sent were coming from and where the packets were going to in the receiving computer. Now that we are looking at the Application layer, we can add the two applications that are the source and the destination of the stream of data.

Let's assume the web browser has made a transport connection to the web server and has started downloading an image file. The web server has opened the image file and is sending the data from the file to its Transport layer as quickly as possible. But the Transport layer must follow the rules of window size, so it can only send a certain amount of data at a time. When the window fills up, the web server is paused until the Transport layer on the destination computer has started to receive and acknowledge packets.

As the Transport layer on the destination computer starts to receive packets, reconstruct the stream of data, and acknowledge packets, it delivers the reconstructed stream of packets to the web browser application display on the user's screen. Sometimes on a slow connection you can see your browser "paint" pictures as the data is downloaded. On a fast connection the data comes so quickly that the pictures appear instantaneously.

If we redraw our picture of packets in the Transport layer, adding both of the application layers where the packets are in the middle of an image, now it looks like this:

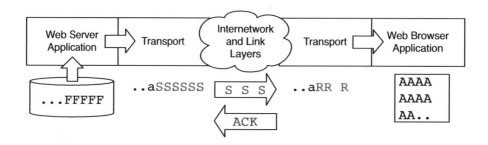

Figure 7.6: Buffering in the Application and Transport Layers

The web server is reading the image file ('F') and sending it as a stream to the web browser as quickly as it can send the data. The source Transport layer has broken the stream into packets and used IP to send the packets to the destination computer.

The Transport layer has sent six packets ('S') and has stopped sending because it has reached its window size and paused the web server. Three of those six packets have made it to the Transport layer on the destination computer ('R') and three of the packets are still making their way across the Internet ('S').

As the destination Transport layer pieces the stream back together, it both sends an acknowledgement (ACK) and delivers the data to the receiving application (the web browser). The web browser reconstructs the image ('A') and displays it to the user as the data is received.

A key thing to notice in this picture is that the transport layers do not keep the packets for the entire file. They only retain packets that are "in transit" and unacknowledged. Once packets are acknowledged and delivered to the destination application, there is no reason for either the source or destination Transport layer to hold on to the packets.

When the acknowledgment flows back from the destination computer to the source computer, the Transport layer on the source computer unpauses the web server application and the web server continues to read data from the file and send it to the source Transport layer for transmission.

This ability to start and stop the sending application to make sure we send data as quickly as possible without sending data so fast that they clog up the Internet is called "flow control". The applications are not responsible for flow control, they just try to send or receive data as quickly as possible and the two transport layers start and stop the applications as needed based on the speed and reliability of the network.

7.6 Writing Networked Applications

The applications which send and receive data over the network are written in one or more programming languages. Many programming languages have libraries of code that make it quite simple to write application code to send and receive data across the network. With a good programming library, making a connection to an application running on a server, sending data to the server, and receiving data from the server is generally as easy as reading and writing a file.

As an example, the code below is all it takes in the Python programming language to make a connection to a web server and retrieve a document:

```
import socket

mysock = socket.socket(socket.AF_INET, socket.SOCK_STREAM)
mysock.connect(('www.py4inf.com', 80))
mysock.send('GET http://www.py4inf.com/code/romeo.txt HTTP/1.0\n\n')

while True:
    data = mysock.recv(512)
    if ( len(data) < 1 ) :
        break
    print data

mysock.close()
```

Figure 7.7: Programming with Sockets in Python

While you may or not know the Python programming language, the key point is that it only takes ten lines of application code to make and use a network connection. This code is simple because the Transport, Internetwork, and Link layers so effectively solve the problems at each of their layers that applications using the network can ignore nearly all of the details of how the network is implemented.

In the Python application, in this line of code

```
mysock.connect(('www.py4inf.com', 80))
```

we have specified that we are connecting to the application that is listening for incoming connections on port 80 on the remote computer www.py4inf.com.

By choosing port 80 we are indicating that we want to connect to a World Wide Web server on that host and are expecting to communicate with that server using the HyperText Transport Protocol.

7.7 Summary

The entire purpose of the lower three layers (Transport, Internetwork, and Link) is to make it so that applications running in the Application layer can focus the application problem that needs to be solved and leave virtually all of the complexity of moving data across a network to be handled by the lower layers of the network model.

Because this approach makes it so simple to build networked applications, we have seen a wide range of networked applications including web browsers, mail applications, networked video games, network-based telephony applications, and many others. And what is even more exciting is that it is easy to experiment and build whole new types of networked applications to solve problems that have not yet been imagined.

7.8 Glossary

HTML: HyperText Markup Language. A textual format that marks up text using tags surrounded by less-than and greater-than characters. Example HTML looks like: <p>This is nice</p>.

HTTP: HyperText Transport Protocol. An Application layer protocol that allows web browsers to retrieve web documents from web servers.

IMAP: Internet Message Access Protocol. A protocol that allows mail clients to log into and retrieve mail from IMAP-enabled mail servers.

flow control: When a sending computer slows down to make sure that it does not overwhelm either the network or the destination computer. Flow control also causes the sending computer to increase the speed at which data is sent when it is sure that the network and destination computer can handle the faster data rates.

socket: A software library available in many programming languages that makes creating a network connection and exchanging data nearly as easy as opening and reading a file on your computer.

status code: One aspect of the HTTP protocol that indicates the overall success or failure of a request for a document. The most well-known HTTP status code is "404", which is how an HTTP server tells an HTTP client (i.e., a browser) that it the requested document could not be found.

telnet: A simple client application that makes TCP connections to various address/port combinations and allows typed data to be sent across the connection. In the early days of the Internet, telnet was used to remotely log in to a computer across the network.

web browser: A client application that you run on your computer to retrieve and display web pages.

web server: An application that deliver (serves up) Web pages

7.9 Questions

You can take this quiz online at http://www.net-intro.com/quiz/

1. Which layer is right below the Application layer?

a) Transport
b) Internetworking
c) Link Layer
d) Obtuse layer

2. What kind of document is used to describe widely used Application layer protocols?

a) DHCP
b) RFC
c) APPDOC
d) ISO 9000

3. Which of these is an idea that was invented in the Application layer?

a) 0f:2a:b3:1f:b3:1a
b) 192.168.3.14
c) www.khanacademy.com
d) http://www.dr-chuck.com/

4. Which of the following is *not* something that the Application layer worries about?

a) Whether the client or server starts talking first
b) The format of the commands and responses exchanged across a socket
c) How the window size changes as data is sent across a socket
d) How data is represented as it is sent across the network to assure interoperability.

5. Which of these is an Application layer protocol?

a) HTTP
b) TCP
c) DHCP
d) Ethernet

6. What port would typically be used to talk to a web server?

a) 23
b) 80
c) 103
d) 143

7. What is the command that a web browser sends to a web server to retrieve an web document?

a) RETR

   b) DOCUMENT
   c) 404
   d) GET

8. What is the purpose of the "Content-type:" header when you retrieve a document over the web protocol?

   a) Tells the browser how to display the retrieved document
   b) Tells the browser where to go if the document cannot be found
   c) Tells the browser whether or not the retrieved document is empty
   d) Tells the browser where the headers end and the content starts

9. What common UNIX command can be used to send simple commands to a web server?

   a) ftp
   b) ping
   c) traceroute
   d) telnet

10. What does an HTTP status code of "404" mean?

   a) Document has moved
   b) Successful document retrieval
   c) Protocol error
   d) Document not found

11. What characters are used to mark up HTML documents?

   a) Less-than and greater-than signs < >
   b) Exclamation points !
   c) Square brackets [ ]
   d) Curly brackets { }

12. What is a common application protocol for retrieving mail?

   a) RFC
   b) HTML

    c) ICANN

    d) IMAP

13. What application protocol does RFC15 describe?

    a) telnet

    b) ping

    c) traceroute

    d) www

14. What happens to a server application that is sending a large file when the TCP layer has sent enough data to fill the window size and has not yet received an acknowledgement?

    a) The application switches its transmission to a new socket

    b) The application crashes and must be restarted

    c) The application is paused until the remote computer acknowledges that it has received some of the data

    d) The closest gateway router starts to discard packets that would exceed the window size

15. What is a "socket" on the Internet?

    a) A way for devices to get wireless power

    b) A way for devices to get an IP address

    c) An entry in a routing table

    d) A two-way data connection between a pair of client and server applications

16. What must an application know to make a socket connection in software?

    a) The address of the server and the port number on the server

    b) The route between the source and destination computers

    c) Which part of the IP address is the network number

    d) The initial size of the TCP window during transmission

Chapter 8

Secure Transport Layer

In the early days of the Internet, networks were small and all of the routers were in secure locations. As long as each computer connected to the Internet protected itself from unwanted incoming connections, it was felt that there was no need to protect data from prying eyes while it was crossing the network.

So the Link, Internetwork, and Transport layers were focused on the efficient movement of data and solving the problems of a large-scale shared distributed network without worrying about the privacy of that data.

But as the use of the Internet grew rapidly in the late 1980s and literally exploded when the Web became mainstream in 1994, security and privacy of network traffic became very important problems to solve. When we began using the Internet to conduct commerce and credit cards and bank account numbers were being routinely sent across the network, securing data became essential. And when we started using wireless technologies like WiFi, security became necessary for even the simplest uses of the Internet.

There are two general approaches to securing network activity. The first makes sure that all of the network hardware (routers and links) is in physically secure locations so it is not possible for someone to sneak in and monitor traffic while it is crossing the Internet. This approach is not practical for hundreds of thousands of network routers owned and operated by many different organizations. While you might be able to ensure that some of the router operators adhered to strict security procedures and policies, sooner or later a mistake will be made. And once WiFi was added to the mix and your packets went over radio waves, a network attacker could just sit in a coffee shop and intercept packets as they passed through the air.

Under these conditions, the only reasonable solution is to encrypt data in your computer before it is sent across its first physical link, and then decrypt the data in the destination computer after it arrives. Using this approach, we assume that an attacker can see all of the packets that you send, but they cannot decrypt the data that they have captured. The encryption also guarantees that there is no way to alter your data while it is crossing the Internet.

8.1   Encrypting and Decrypting Data

The concept of protecting information so it cannot be read while it is being transported over an insecure medium is thousands of years old. The leaders in Roman armies sent coded messages to each other using a code called the "Caesar Cipher". The simplest version of this approach is to take each of the characters of the actual message (we call this "plain text") and shift each character a fixed distance down the alphabet to produce the scrambled message or "ciphertext".

Then we send the ciphertext via the courier or other insecure transport to the other person. The courier cannot read the message because it appears to be random characters unless you know the technique used to encode the message.

As long as the person receiving the message knew the number used to shift the message, they could unshift the characters in the encoded message to reproduce the original message.

Here is a simple example of plain text and ciphertext using a shift of one:

```
Plain text:  Go to the river
Cipher text: Hp up uif sjwfs
```

We user the word "encrypt" to describe transforming the plain text to the ciphertext and "decrypt" to describe the reverse process.

The Caesar Cipher is very simple to defeat, but it was used to protect important messages until about 150 years ago. Modern encryption techniques are far more sophisticated than a simple character shift, but all encryption systems depend on some kind of a secret key that both parties are aware of so they can decrypt received data.

8.2 Two Kinds of Secrets

The traditional way to encrypt transmissions is using a shared secret that only the sending and receiving parties know. With the secret, it is easy to decrypt the received data, but if you received the data without possessing the secret, it would be effectively impossible to decrypt the message.

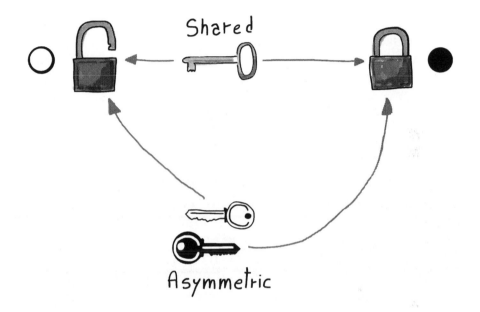

Figure 8.1: Shared Versus Asymmetric Keys

In the early days of the Internet, two people could send encrypted email to each other by one person first calling the other person on the phone and giving them the decryption secret. This worked well when there were only a few users on the network, but could not scale to situations where a company might have millions of customers and could not afford to make a phone call to each customer to establish a shared secret before they could make a purchase.

It might seem like a good idea to distribute the shared secrets over the Internet, but if we assume that the attackers are monitoring and capturing all network traffic, they could also capture the unencrypted message that contained the shared secret. At that point it would be trivial for the attacker to use the shared secret to decrypt a message. And even worse, the attacker could intercept a message, delay it, then decrypt it, change and re-encrypt it, and send the modified message back on its way. The receiving computer would decrypt the message and never know that it had been modified by an attacker while in transit.

So shared secrets clearly would not work to solve the problem of securing network traffic between trillions of pairs of networked computers.

The solution to this problem came in the 1970s when the concept of asymmetric key encryption was developed. The idea of asymmetric key encryption is that one key is used to encrypt the message and another key is used to decrypt it. The computer that will be receiving the encrypted data chooses both the encryption key and decryption key. Then the encryption key is sent to the computer that will be sending the data. The sending computer encrypts the data and sends it across the network. The receiving computer uses the decryption key to decrypt the data.

We call the encryption key the "public" key because it is can be widely shared. We call the decryption key the "private" key because it never leaves the computer where it was created. Another name for asymmetric keys is public/private keys.

The whole process is designed so that if an attacker has the public key (which was sent unencrypted) and the encrypted text, it is virtually impossible to decrypt the encrypted data. There is a lot of math with large prime numbers that makes it hard to guess the private key from the public key and encrypted data.

So with the advent of public/private key technology, the only question left was how to apply it in our network model.

8.3   Secure Sockets Layer (SSL)

Since network engineers decided to add security nearly 20 years after the Internet protocols were developed, it was important not to break any existing Internet protocols or architecture. Their solution was to add an optional partial layer between the Transport layer and the Application layer. They called this partial layer the Secure Sockets Layer (SSL) or Transport Layer Security (TLS).

When an application requested that the Transport layer make a connection to a remote host, it could request that the connection either be encrypted or unencrypted. If an encrypted connection was requested, the Transport layer encrypted the data before breaking the stream into packets. This meant that the Transport layer, Internetwork layer, and physical (link) layers could still perform exactly the same way whether the packets were encrypted

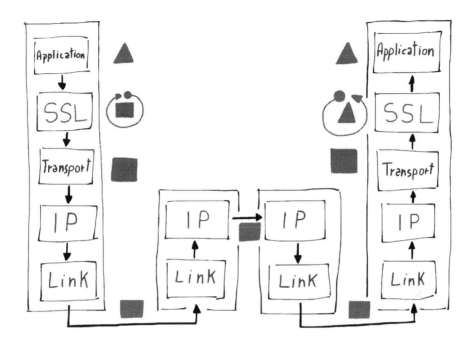

Figure 8.2: Where Encryption and Decryption Happens

or non-encrypted. The applications making the connections were also spared the details of how encryption and decryption worked.

Since encryption was a simple and transparent addition to the Transport layer, there was no need to change the routers that operate at the Internetwork and Link layers. There was no need to change any Link layer hardware to make encryption work. And applications did not need to be modified except to request that a connection be encrypted when appropriate.

8.4 Encrypting Web Browser Traffic

Since web browsers and web servers operate at the application layer, we barely notice whether we are using encrypted or un-encrypted connections. Web browsers use the URL convention of replacing "http:" with "https:" to indicate that the browser is to communicate with the web server using the Secure Transport Layer instead of the unencrypted Transport layer. Your browser will usually show a "lock" icon in the address bar to let you know that you are communicating with a secure web site.

There is a small overhead in setting up the https connections and a small cost to encrypt and decrypt the data that is being sent. Since https was slightly more costly, for a while it was used only for pages that contained passwords, bank account numbers, or other sensitive data.

But over time as networks have become faster and the https implementations have gotten much more efficient, there is a trend toward encrypting all web server interactions whenever you are interacting with a web server where you have an account. The current trend is towards using https for all web traffic.

8.5   Certificates and Certificate Authorities

While public/private key encryption works to allow the distribution of encryption keys across insecure networks and the use of those keys to encrypt transmissions, there is still a problem of knowing if the public key that you have received when you connected to a server is really from the organization it claims to be from.

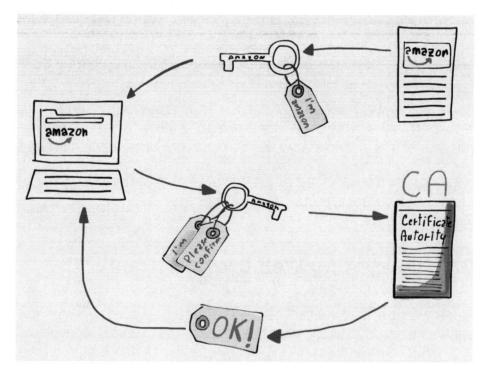

Figure 8.3: Certificate Authorities and Public Keys

Perhaps you think you are connecting to www.amazon.com but a rogue computer intercepts your traffic, claiming to be www.amazon.com and giving you a public key to use for encryption. If your web browser trusts the key, it will use the rogue computer's public key to encrypt your banking information and send it to the rogue computer. Since the rogue computer gave you the public key, it also has the corresponding private key and is able to decrypt and abscond with your banking information.

So your computer needs to know who the key is actually coming from. This is achieved by sending you a public key that is digitally signed by a Certificate Authority (CA). When your computer or browser is initially installed, it knows about a number of well-known certificate authorities. If your browser is given a public key that is signed by one of the well-known certificate authorities, it trusts the key and uses it to encrypt and send your data. If your computer receives a public key that is not signed by one of its trusted certificate authorities, it will warn you before sending your data using the key.

If you see a warning message about an untrusted certificate, you should probably say "no" and figure out why your network traffic is not being routed to the server that you think it is going to before sending any sensitive data.

8.6 Summary

Since the Internet was nearly 20 years old before we needed broadly deployed security, we had to find a way to add security to the already existing four-layer model. The perfect place to add security was as an option in the Transport layer. This is why we call secure connections on the Internet "Secure Sockets Layer" (SSL) or "Transport Layer Security" (TLS). There are subtle differences between SSL and TLS but they both encrypt data at the Transport layer.

The invention of public/private key encryption was well timed in that it solved the key distribution problem of shared-secret encryption approaches. With public/private keys, the public encryption key can be routinely shared across insecure media. This means we can use an unencrypted connection to exchange data and upgrade the connection to a secure connection.

By inserting the secure layer at the top of the Transport layer, we were able to avoid changing the Application, Internetwork, and Link layers while still easily securing any Transport layer connection. This approach ensures that all data being sent across a connection is encrypted before it leaves your computer. Given that many of us use wireless connections like WiFi, which are easily monitored by attackers, it is a good idea to encrypt data before it is sent across WiFi.

Browsers support secure connections by changing the prefix on the URL from "http:" to "https:". By keeping an eye on the URL, end users can make sure they never send sensitive data across insecure connections. A series of trusted Certificate Authorities will sign public keys to give you an assurance that the key you received is indeed from the organization you expect it to be.

The design of the Secure Transport Layer provides a secure and yet easy-to-use mechanism for secure communications across the Internet at a scale of trillions of pairs of interacting computers.

8.7 Glossary

asymmetric key: An approach to encryption where one (public) key is used to encrypt data prior to transmission and a different (private) key is used to decrypt data once it is received.

certificate authority: An organization that digitally signs public keys after verifying that the name listed in the public key is actually the person or organization in possession of the public key.

ciphertext: A scrambled version of a message that cannot be read without knowing the decryption key and technique.

decrypt: The act of transforming a ciphertext message to a plain text message using a secret or key.

encrypt: The act of transforming a plain text message to a ciphertext message using a secret or key.

plain text: A readable message that is about to be encrypted before being sent.

private key: The portion of a key pair that is used to decrypt transmissions.

public key: The portion of a key pair that is used to encrypt transmissions.

shared secret: An approach to encryption that uses the same key for encryption and decryption.

SSL: Secure Sockets Layer. An approach that allows an application to request that a Transport layer connection is to be encrypted as it crosses the network. Similar to Transport Layer Security (TLS).

TLS: Transport Layer Security. An approach that allows an application to request that a Transport layer connection is to be encrypted as it crosses the network. Similar to Secure Sockets Layer (SSL).

8.8 Questions

You can take this quiz online at http://www.net-intro.com/quiz/

1. How do we indicate that we want a secure connection when using a web browser?

   a) Use https:// in the URL
   b) Use a secure web browser
   c) Open an incognito window
   d) Manually encode the address of the server using SHA1

2. Why is a shared-secret approach not suitable for use on the Internet?

   a) Because people would lose or misplace the secret
   b) It is difficult to distribute the secrets
   c) Encryption and decryption with shared secrets are too easily broken
   d) Encryption and decryption with shared secrets take too much compute power

3. What is the underlying mathematical concept that makes public/private key encryption secure?

   a) Continuous functions
   b) Taylor series
   c) Karnaugh Maps
   d) Prime numbers

4. Which of the keys can be sent across the Internet in plain text without compromising security?

a) Encryption key
b) Decryption Key
c) Shared Secret
d) Univerally Safe Key (USK)

5. Where does the Secure Sockets Layer (SSL) fit in the four-layer Internet architecture?

a) Below the Link layer
b) Between the Link and Internetworking layers
c) Between the Internetworking and Transport layers
d) Between the Transport and Application layers

6. If you were properly using https in a browser over WiFi in a cafe, which of the following is the greatest risk to your losing credit card information when making an online purchase?

a) Someone captured the packets that were sent across the WiFi
b) Someone captured the packets in the gateway router
c) Someone captured the packets as they passed through a core Intenet router
d) You have a virus on your computer that is capturing keystrokes

7. With the Secure Sockets Layer, where are packets encrypted and decrypted?

a) They are encrypted and decrypted as they pass through the router
b) Each physical link has its own separate encryption
c) They are encrypted in your computer and decrypted in the server
d) They are encrypted in the WiFi gateway and decrypted in the last router before the destination computer

8. What changes to the IP layer were needed to make secure socket layer (SSL) work?

a) No changes were needed
b) We had to add support for Secure IP (IPSEC)
c) We needed to support longer packets in IP

d) The Time-To-Live (TTL) value needed to be encrypted

9. If a rogue element was able to monitor all packets going through an undersea cable and you were using pub-lic/private key encryption properly, which of the following would be the most difficult for them to obtain?

   a) What servers you were communicating with
   b) How often you used the servers
   c) How much data you retrieved from the servers
   d) Which documents you retrieved from the servers

10. What is the purpose of a Certificate Authority in pub-lic/private key encryption?

    a) To make sure people do not forge badges for learning activi-ties
    b) To make sure packets get routed to the correct destination computer
    c) To assure us that a public key comes from the organization it claims to be from
    d) To choose when a particular country must switch from IPv4 to IPv6

11. The ARPANET network was in operation starting in the 1960s. Secure Sockets Layer (SSL) was not invented util the 1980s. How did the ARPANET insure the security of the data on its network?

    a) By using public/private keys and encrypting all transmis-sions
    b) By using encryption at the Link layer
    c) By making sure no one could access the physical links
    d) By only using secure WiFi routers

12. Which of these answers is "Security is fun" encrypted with a Caesar Cipher shift of 1.

    a) Ptsjduao rt dii
    b) Wentudhs di dju
    c) Tfdvsjuz jt gvo
    d) Asdfghjk qw zxc

13. What Caesar Cipher shift was used to encrypt "V yvxr fr-phevgl"?

   a) 1
   b) 6
   c) 13
   d) 24

Chapter 9

The OSI Model

So far we have spent all of our time describing the four-layer model used to design and implement the TCP/IP protocols and applications that make up the Internet. However, the TCP/IP model is not the only model we can use to help us understand how networks work. The other model commonly used to make sense of network design is called the Open System Interconnection (OSI) model. While the TCP/IP model was designed and evolved as the TCP/IP protocols were developed, deployed, and changed, the OSI model was the result of a careful design process by many networking experts who worked to develop a general approach to network models.

In today's networked world, the OSI model and the TCP/IP model serve two different purposes.[1] The TCP/IP model is an *implementation* model, in that it provides the guidance for those who would build TCP/IP-compatible network hardware or software. The OSI model is more of an *abstract* model that can be used to understand a wide range of network architectures.

While TCP/IP is the most widely used network technology today, many different types of networks have been implemented and deployed over the past 50 years. And as we continue to improve and evolve networking, new implementation models may emerge.

The OSI model has seven layers instead of the four layers of the TCP/IP model. Starting at the bottom (nearest the physical connections) of the OSI model, the layers are: (1) Physical, (2) Data Link, (3) Network, (4) Transport, (5) Session, (6) Presentation, and

---

[1]This, of course, is an oversimplification. Prior to 1990, there *were* operational network implementations based on ISO specifications that followed the OSI network model very closely. But today, those ISO/OSI network implementations no longer are in broad use.

(7) Application. We will look at each layer in the OSI model in turn, starting with the Physical layer.

9.1 Physical (Layer 1)

The OSI Physical layer deals with the physical attributes of the actual wired, wireless, fiber optic, or other connection that is used to transport data across a single link. The Physical layer also defines the shapes of the connectors and type of media which can be used. Another problem solved at this layer is how to encode the bits (0's and 1's) that make up the data being sent across the medium.[2] The "bit encoding" (or modulation) determines how fast data can be sent across the link.

9.2 Data Link (Layer 2)

The OSI Data Link layer is concerned with how the systems using a physical link cooperate with one another. When data is broken into packets, the Data Link layer defines special sequences to indicate the beginning and end of each packet. The stations communicating using the physical connection are assigned addresses to allow for effective use of the media. Sometimes multiple stations are sharing the same media (as on a wireless network) and the Data Link layer defines how those stations will share the connections with the other systems connected to the network. Most Data Link layers also have some form of checksum to detect and/or correct for errors in the transmitted data.

The design problems solved in the Physical and Data Link layers of the OSI model are addressed by the Link layer of the TCP/IP model.

9.3 Network (Layer 3)

Like the Internetwork Layer (IP) in the TCP/IP model, the OSI Network layer deals with the global assignment of "routable" addresses to the various systems connected to the network. The

---

[2]"Manchester Encoding" is a common technique for encoding bits for transmission across a wire.

Network layer governs how routers forward packets across multiple hops to get from their source to their destination. Like the IP layer, The OSI Network layer does not attempt to be error free, as it assumes that lost data will be detected and retransmitted at the next layer up.

9.4 Transport (Layer 4)

The Transport layer in the OSI model manages packet loss and retransmission as well as flow control and window size. The rest of the functionality of the TCP/IP Transport layer is handled in the Session layer in the OSI model.

9.5 Session (Layer 5)

The OSI Session layer handles establishing connections between applications. The Session layer deals with "ports" so that a connecting client application can "find" the correct server application on a particular system. Some aspects of secure transmission are also handled in the OSI Session layer.

9.6 Presentation (Layer 6)

The Presentation layer focuses on how data is represented and encoded for transmission across the network. As an example, the Presentation layer would describe how to encode the pixels of an image so that the receiving application can properly decode the data. The Presentation layer also handles data encryption and decryption.

9.7 Application (Layer 7)

The OSI Application Layer is very similar to the Application layer in the TCP/IP model, in that it contains the applications themselves. Some applications are client applications that initiate connections, and other applications are the server applications that respond to those connection requests. The various pairs of applications have protocol standards that define interoperability between multiple clients and multiple servers from different vendors.

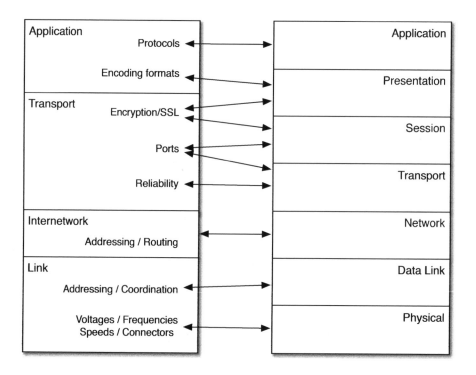

Figure 9.1: Comparing the TCP and OSI Models

9.8   Comparing the OSI and TCP/IP Models

We can use the OSI model to provide an alternative "view" of the TCP/IP model by comparing how the OSI model breaks network functionality into its layers and how the TCP/IP model breaks its functionality into layers.

9.9   Link Layer (TCP/IP)

The TCP/IP Link layer combines the Physical and Data Link layers from the OSI model. The Physical and Data Link layers are usually implemented in hardware. Products like Ethernet, WiFi, satellite, or fiber optic often are implemented in a network driver card that plugs into the back of a computer or router. The network driver card generally implements both the physical and the data link aspects of the connection in the hardware on the card. In most cases, the data link layers are tuned to the limitations and requirements of their corresponding physical layers. So in real systems, it is somewhat rare for a particular data link layer to be arbitrarily paired with any number of physical layers. Since it can be hard to separate the physical and data link aspects for a particular link technology, the TCP model combines them into a single layer for simplicity.

9.10   Internetwork Layer (TCP/IP)

One place that maps pretty cleanly between the two models is the OSI Network and TCP/IP Internetwork layers. They perform the same functions of creating a globally routable address space and building routers to insure that packets properly find their way from the source to the destination across multiple hops.

9.11   Transport Layer (TCP/IP)

The features of the Transport layer in TCP/IP are spread across the Transport and Session layers of the OSI model. The OSI Transport layer deals with flow control and packet retransmission, while the OSI Presentation layer deals with multiple applications running on multiple ports as well as session establishment and teardown.

The Secure Sockets Layer (SSL) in the TCP/IP model corresponds to parts of the Session and Presentation layers in the OSI model.

9.12   Application Layer (TCP/IP)

The TCP/IP Application Layer combines the non-security aspects of the OSI Presentation layer and the OSI Application layer. While many TCP/IP applications deal with issues like encoding and decoding various types of data, the TCP/IP model does not see data formatting as a separate "layer". Various data encoding and decoding technologies are used in TCP/IP applications, but TCP/IP tends to treat these capabilities as library code that applications make use of as needed for the application.

9.13 Conclusion

While the TCP/IP model described in this book is widely used to guide the implementation of TCP/IP networks, hardware, and software, the OSI model can help us look at and compare a wide range of network architectures ranging from openly developed networks to proprietary vendor-specific networks.

9.14 Glossary

abstract model: A model and set of terminology that is used to generally understand a problem area and guide the development of standards and implementations to solve problems.

implementation model: A model and set of terminology that is used to guide the development of standards and an implementation to solve a particular problem.

ISO: International Organization for Standardization. A worldwide body that develops standards in computing, networking, and many other areas.

OSI: Open System Interconnection. A seven-layer model used to help organize the design of various approaches to network architecture.

9.15 Questions

You can take this quiz online at http://www.net-intro.com/quiz/

1. What is the primary value of the OSI network model?

a) OSI networks are used in the southern hemisphere
b) The OSI approach can be use to analyze many different network models
c) OSI networks make better use of limited bandwidth
d) OSI networks are more secure

2. How many layers does the OSI model have?

a) Four

b) Six
c) Seven
d) Nine

3. Which of the OSI layers deals with the shape of connectors for network connections?

a) Physical
b) Data Link
c) Network
d) Transport

4. Which of the layers is most similar between the OSI and TCP network models?

a) TCP Link Layer and OSI Data Link Layer
b) TCP Internetwork Layer and OSI Network Layer
c) TCP Transport Layer and OSI Transport Layer
d) TCP Application Layer and OSI Session Layer

5. What layer does the TCP/IP Secure Sockets Layer map to in the OSI network model?

a) Secure Data Link Layer (SDLL)
b) Secure Network Layer (SNL)
c) Secure Transport Layer (STL)
d) Session and Presentation Layers

6. Why does the TCP model combine the OSI Data Link and Physical layers into a single Link layer?

a) Because the TCP model does not worry about the Physical layer
b) Because the TCP model designers were ignored at the 1981 OSI meeting in Utrect, Netherlands
c) Because quite often the design of Data Link and Physical layers are tightly connected for a particular technology
d) To make the TCP model easier to understand by end users

Chapter 10

Wrap Up

It has been said that building the Internet solved the world's most complex engineering problem to date. The design and engineering of the Internet started well over 50 years ago. It has been continuously improving and evolving over the past 50 years and will continue to evolve in the future.

The Internet now connects billions of computers using many thousands of routers and link-level connections. The Internet is so complex that it is never fully operational, The Internet is less about being "perfect" and more about adapting to problems, outages, errors, lost data, and many other unforeseen problems. The Internet is designed to be flexible and adapt to whatever problems are encountered.

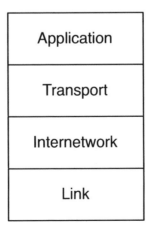

Figure 10.1: The Four-Layer Model

In order to build an overall solution that works at scale, it was important to break the Internet engineering problems down into four distinct layers:

- The Link/Physical layer includes all of the complex engineering required to move data across a single "hop", whether the hop is a wireless WiFi, wired Ethernet, fiber optic, or satellite connection.

- The Internetwork Protocol (IP) layer is how data is routed across a series of hops to get quickly and efficiently from one of a billion source computers to any of a billion destination computers. The IP layer dynamically adjusts and reroutes data based on network load, link performance, or network outages. While the IP layer is highly reliable and fast, at times it loses or even throws away data. The IP layer is not responsible for insuring the overall reliability of the network. It just moves the data the best that it can.

- The Transport layer compensates for any imperfections in the IP or Link layers. The Transport layer makes sure that any lost packets are retransmitted and packets that arrive out of order are put back into order before being passed on to the receiving application. The Transport layer also acts as flow control between the sending and receiving applications to make sure that data is moved quickly when the network is fast and the links are not overloaded, and to slow the transfer of data when using slower or heavily loaded links. The data flow and rate limitation in the Transport layer allow the Internet to continue to function smoothly even when it is heavily loaded.

- The other three layers make the use of the network very simple for the Application Layer. An application can make a network connection and send/receive data on that connection with just a few lines of code. By making the use of the network simple, applications can focus on solving the end-user problems they need to solve. Because it is so easy for applications to use the network in new and different ways, we have seen the emergence of a wide range of highly innovative applications that work without any changes required to the Internet protocols.

Without breaking the problem of engineering and building the Internet into these four distinct layers, it would be far more difficult to build and deploy ever-improving versions of the network. And if every single application needed to be fully aware of all of the complex details required to use the Internet, it would greatly limit the richness and diversity of the networked applications that we have today.

It is amazing to realize what has been accomplished in building the Internet over the past 50 years. But in a way, we have only just begun the engineering journey of building networked applications. It does not take much to imagine an Internet where every light switch, lightbulb, refrigerator, table, automobile, roadway, flying drone, and chair has an Internet address and they all want to communicate with one another. New engineering issues will have to be solved, and perhaps even the four-layer network model will need to evolve to meet these new engineering challenges.

But just like brilliant engineers designed and evolved network protocols to move from hundreds of network-connected computers to billions of network-connected computers, our present and future engineers will certainly solve the problems and challenges we will face as the network evolves to connect trillions of computers.

Index